THE FREEDOM OF LOVE

THE FREEDOM OF LOVE

Rafael de Santiago

GRACEWING

First published in England in 2012
by
Gracewing
2 Southern Avenue
Leominster
Herefordshire HR6 0QF
United Kingdom
www.gracewing.co.uk

ISBN 978 085244 779 6

Typeset by Gracewing

Contents

Preface

Love is one of those concepts whose meaning we all think we know... until we need to explain it to others. When we try to do so, we realize that the word "love" has so many meanings that it is very difficult to know what true love is.

> *True love is the greatest thing in the world. Except for a nice MLT; a mutton, lettuce, and tomato sandwich, where the mutton is nice and lean, and the tomato is ripe.* (Miracle Max, *The Princess Bride*).

The aim of this book is to provide the reader with a clear understanding of what true love is, as well as its relationship to freedom. The ideas that are presented in the following pages apply to sexual love, but they also apply to friendship, to the love of parents for their children, of children for their parents, etc. Married couples, those who are engaged, and those who are looking for a spouse, as well as those who are single by choice, will find that the ideas contained in this book apply to them. Love is man's highest calling, and it is something we all long for.

Introduction

If you believe you can fly and you jump off a high cliff to prove it, you will fall to your death because people cannot fly. This is a dramatic example of how an incorrect understanding of human nature can lead to a disastrous end.

An incorrect understanding of what a human being is can also lead people to live unhappy lives. This is so because the way we live largely depends on the concept we have of what a person is. The following pages are based on two principles about the human being. The first one is that:

Man is the only animal that can have and give.

A person can have material possessions, but he can also have ideas, desires, feelings, fears, emotions, and virtues. "Having" opens up the subjective dimension of the person. The second principle is that:

Man is made for giving.

Both having and giving are important parts of our development as persons. Having is not the "bad guy," and giving is not the "good." Both are good, although giving is more important than having. Because this is not obvious, in Chapter 4 it is argued that man develops as a person when he makes a complete gift of himself.

The reference point of this book is the dignity of the human being. If you drive through a red light and you are stopped by the police, you may try to argue with the officer that you do not believe in traffic lights, or that you did not feel bad when you drove through the red light, or that you are not sure about the existence of those laws... but you will not avoid getting a ticket. You may not like the traffic laws, but this does not mean that they do not apply to you. You may not feel bad when you disobey the traffic laws, but the way you feel does not modify those laws.

Who the person is has certain implications for the way we behave. For example, we would all like to fly to avoid traffic on the freeways, but the truth is that we do not fly. You may not like this law and decide to jump off the cliff, but the fact that humans do not fly still applies to you—as you would quickly discover.

In the same way, there are also laws that govern the behavior of human beings with regard to love and the use of our freedom. You may not like these laws, but they still apply to you. Disobeying the physical laws has consequences that we can grasp with our senses, but disobeying the laws that regulate the use of our freedom, or those that regulate the development of true love, do not necessarily have an external impact on us. Their main impact is internal; they affect the core of who we are.

This book is roughly divided into two parts. In the first (Chapters 1 to 7) we introduce the basic ideas and we set the stage for the second part (Chapters 8 to 10), in which we explore some of the deeper aspects of the gift of self.

The first part of this book may seem too simple, so the reader should be careful that this apparent simplicity does not distract his or her attention from two basic ideas: the notion of the gift of self (Chapter 4) and the nuptial meaning of the body (Chapter 5). In the last chapters the tone becomes more philosophical. Although these chapters require more attention, your effort will be rewarded with a deeper understanding of what true love is.

In the following pages "man" generally means "humanity." When it refers only to the male members of humanity it will be clear from the context. Given the reciprocity of the love between a man and a woman, if one did not use this inclusive language, the text would be full of expressions so difficult to follow that the readers—both females and males—would be bored to death. For example, if one had to express with non-inclusive language the following idea:

> *When man gives himself completely he surrenders his own will to the beloved, in the sense that he limits his freedom on behalf of the person whom he loves,*

one would have to say:

> *When man or woman gives himself or herself completely he or she surrenders his or her own will to the beloved, in the sense that he or she limits his or her freedom on behalf of the person whom he or she loves.*

I believe that injustices against women are not overcome by making the language cumbersome. I am sure that the reader will find it more respectful of his (or her) time if the text can be easily understood by all.

This book was written in San Diego, California, over a period of several years. When it was almost finished I moved to Barcelona, where I made minor corrections, polished a few things here and there, and translated the English manuscript into Spanish. Although the Spanish translation was published first, what you have in your hands is basically the original work. The feedback that I received from the Spanish version has led me to streamline some arguments and eliminate others altogether. Fortunately for the English reader, the book has become shorter and—I hope—easier to read.

Throughout this process I have been fortunate enough to count on the help and advice of many friends. Peter Weiss, Jim Baker, and Mark Murphy read the first manuscripts and did substantial work to help me turn those original drafts into a readable text. I owe them a special debt of gratitude. I am grateful to Amanda Shaw for her help in editing the original text, and to Michael Stonehouse for his comments and his patience with the drawings. Janet Weiss, Sebastien Brion, Ted Villaseñor, John Twist, and Ana Vericat helped improve successive versions of the text. I would also like to thank Ines Stonehouse and Rosemary Sporleder for their help. My gratitude extends as well to the publishers at Gracewing, who have provided valuable suggestions and have assisted me in so many ways. The greatest debt of gratitude, however, is to my parents, who taught me from a young age the meaning of true love.

I hope this book will help many people give themselves completely, as well as understand the beauty of what they are doing. To make a complete gift of one's self is not easy, but that is, in fact, where happiness lies.

CHAPTER 1

What Is Love?

1.1 The Person and His Actions

A dog cannot refer to itself as an "I". Neither can a camel. Man, however, can refer to himself as an "I". When a person reflects on himself, he discovers an inner world of ideas, emotions, desires, feelings, hopes, longings, doubts, fears, joys, puzzlement, forgiveness, amusement, admiration, shame, depression, generosity, disappointments, fantasies, loves, rejections, opinions, anxieties, hostilities, affections, dreams, aspirations, and expectations. It is because of this inner life that man is a person.

If someone were to ask, "What are you?" you would probably say that you are a person. If someone were to ask, "Who are you?" you would probably answer, "I am Tom." The one who asks could add, "Fine, but tell me what makes you Tom, tell me what makes you who you are." In this case, the answer cannot be put into words. There is something at the core of ourselves that defines our subjectivity and that cannot be expressed with words.

This subjectivity makes each person unique and unrepeatable. We can describe to a friend some traits of our character, but no description can exhaust the core of our person. The person is incommunicable.

Objects do not have inner life. Lemonade, umbrellas, and computers are defined by their physical and chemical characteristics. Persons are not defined exclusively by these characteristics; there is something that makes people different from objects, something that sets the person apart from the rest of the things that we know. This something is man's subjectivity, the fact that man is an "I", and this is the foundation of his dignity. This dignity is not a religious fact, in the sense that it does not depend on the religious convictions of the person. It is something that stems from the fact that man can refer to himself as an "I".

If we were angels, our inner life would completely define who we were, but we are humans, so we also need a body. For example, in order to communicate our ideas to others we need to do so with words; something so intimate to us as our ideas cannot be expressed without the body. When a baby is hungry, he cries; if the baby did not cry, he would not be able to communicate his desire for food.

The same happens with our emotions, our desires, our feelings, and our loves. In order to express any single aspect of our inner life we need our body. In the same way that there is a language of words, there is also a language of the body, made up of the way we talk, the way we laugh, the way we dance, the way we act, the way we dress, the way we walk, and so on.

Think of the principal of a school who says, "As I have already expressed my congratulations to the seniors, and they know how proud I am of them, who cares about my manner of dress?" And he goes to the graduation ceremony wearing shorts and a T-shirt. Would the seniors think that he is really proud of them? Note that the principal said, "They know how proud I am of them." These words verbally have an element of truth, but something is missing. If we were angels, it would be enough to express our intentions and good will with our minds, but we are humans and we also have a body. Whatever aspect of our inner life we want to express, we need to express it with our body.

1.2 To Love

If someone asks you what true love is, the question is difficult to answer because the word "love" has many different meanings.

- One may say, "I love Coke" or "I love my job," or we may see a bumper sticker with "I ♡ NY." In these examples "love" means that we like to drink Coke, or that we like our job, or that we like New York City.

- We may also say, "I love my parents," or "I love my cousin Jonathan." In this case we are saying that we feel affection for them.

- We may also say, "It is great to be with my friends; I love my friends." Here "love" means friendship.[1]

- When someone says, "I am in love," this refers to a mixture of physical attraction, sexual desire, and intense feelings.

- We also say that we love God, or that God loves us.

With so many different meanings, it is difficult to say which one is true love. In order to find an answer, we first need to analyze the different types of love.

Think of a little girl who feels lonely or frightened and runs to her mother's arms. She goes to her mother because she loves her, but this love arises from need. She needs her mother. This kind of love we call *need-love*.[2] Many of our loves are need-loves. We have been created in such a way that we need others in order to develop as persons. The husband loves his wife, and at the same time he needs her; the son loves his parents, and at the same time he needs them; we love our friends, and we also need them.

Steve is planning to play golf on Saturday, but his ten-year-old son has a soccer game that morning. He says, "Because I love my son, I will give up golf and I will drive him to the soccer game, and I will watch him play." This is not need-love, for Steve does not need to bring his son to the game. He is giving up something that he would like to do in order to help his son. This type of love we call *gift-love.*

Vince wants to go to the football game on Sunday, but his wife wants to go shopping. He says to himself, "Because I love my wife, I will give up the football game and I will go shopping with her." Vince does not need to go shopping with her. He is giving up something that he would like to do in order to please her. This is sacrificial love, or gift-love.

When John is ready to watch an interesting show on TV, his best friend Alan calls saying that he needs help with something urgent. John says to himself, "As Alan is my friend, I will give up the TV show and go to his house to give him a hand." This is not need-love, for John does not need to help his friend. He is giving up something that he would like to do in order to help his friend.

These latter examples share a common action, namely, to seek the good of the other person. This is precisely the key characteristic of true love. From these examples we can conclude that true love is gift-love. True love is not just wishing for another's good, it is actively willing his good.

> True love is to willingly seek the good of the other.

All the need-loves that we experience (like the affection of a mother for her children, the affection of a son for his parents, the attraction of a young man to his girlfriend, the friendship of a woman with her friends, or the affection of a husband for his wife) can be raised to the level of true love provided we seek the good of the other person.

Our love is always a mixture of need-love and gift-love. Love is a single reality with two different dimensions. It is important to emphasize that our love is not true when we suppress or repress our need-loves. It is true when we raise our need-loves to the level of gift-love (when we seek the good of the other person). The unique reality of our love must have both dimensions in order to be truly human.

1.3   To Love and to Use

Love becomes interesting when we love a person. When we say that we love a thing, we just mean that we like it. When I say, "I love wine," I am just saying that I like wine. I am not seeking the wine's good—rather I am seeking to drink it. When we love a person, we love another "I", another being with an inner life that defines who he is.

We can have a car, a house, a computer, a dog, or a camel. However, we cannot have a person because each person is his own master. The key element of the inner life that defines a person is freedom (no one can choose for me), so we cannot have a person as we have or possess a thing.

Let us now look at how we use the things that we have. We can use a computer to send an e-mail, we can use a bicycle to get to the mall faster, and we can use lemonade to quench our thirst. In these cases we are using an object as a means to an end. However, we cannot rightly use a person as a means to an end because a person is an "I", and we cannot have an "I" as we have a thing.

If we do not respect a person's inner life, then we are treating him as if he were an object. If we were to force a friend to do something against his will, we would not be respecting his freedom and, therefore, we would not be treating him as a person, but rather as an object. If we were to lie to someone in order to get something from him, we would not be respecting his dignity, and we would be using him as an instrument.

We say that a CEO uses his employees as a means to his own ends (to increase the company's profit), and we say that an Army general uses his troops as a means to his own ends (to win the battle). But in these cases "to use" does not mean to use as an object. Assuming the CEO is paying them a fair salary, he is respecting his employees' dignity. In this case, they are all freely pursuing the same goal, the company's goal; the CEO is coordinating their talents and efforts, but they are all working voluntarily and their dignity is being respected. Assuming the Army general is not being reckless, his soldiers' dignity is being respected; the general is coordinating their efforts and skills in order to achieve the common goal.

Of course, there can be cases when a CEO does not respect his employees' dignity, or when a general makes decisions that do not respect his soldiers' dignity. The point is that we ought to respect the dignity of those with whom we interact. When we do not, we use them as objects.

A person can never (rightly) be used as a means to another person's end. We can use the rest of creation for our own sake, but not another person. When a person does not respect the dignity of another, their relationship cannot be true love. This is so because the former would be treating the latter as an object, and objects are things that we have, while true love is gift-love.

True love can only exist when we seek the good of the other (like the dad who gives up golf in order to take his son to the soccer game). The truly human way of interacting with others is to give ourselves to them. If we seek to "have" them in any way, we are using them as a means to our own ends.

Notes

[1] In common language the word "love" tends to be associated with sexual love, and it may sound strange to apply "love" to friendship. But friendship is different than having "buddies" or acquaintances. In fact, friendship is one of the highest forms of love. We will come back to this in Section 4.2.

[2] See the first chapter of C.S. Lewis, *The Four Loves* (New York: Harcout, 1960).

CHAPTER 2

Love and Feelings

2.1 Kindness and Feelings

In the first part of this chapter we look at some realities that are not love, but are often confused with love. An initial mistake is to confuse true love with kindness, which is the desire to relieve another's discomfort or suffering. It may go together with true love, or it may not.

For example, if your brother wants to commit suicide by jumping off a bridge, you leave kindness aside and shout, yell, and physically force him to stop. You are not being kind to your brother, but you are showing true love. You are seeking his good.

When parents have to punish a child, they may not be kind, but they are seeking his good. They are teaching the child important lessons and habits that he would otherwise never learn. Kindness is not the same as true love. They may go together, but they are not the same thing.

The most common mistake today, however, is to confuse true love with feelings, which are states of our inner life. We can feel happy, tired, overwhelmed, euphoric, desperate, or joyful. We can feel grief because a relative died; anger because something went wrong; or compassion for a friend who lost his job. To simplify terminology, we will use the term "sentimentality" as an umbrella to refer to feelings, sentiments, and emotions.

The first point to consider is that, generally speaking, we are not responsible for our feelings. This is so because we cannot help how we feel.[1] John is a San Diego Chargers fan (his team's archrival is the Oakland Raiders), and one day he meets some new friends. If one of them says that he is a Raiders fan, this will generate in John some feelings or emotions. He may not know anything else about him, but John cannot help experiencing a certain feeling toward him.

Anna likes watercolor painting. One day she meets someone who also likes watercolors. This will generate in Anna some positive feelings or emotions. She may not know anything else about the person, but Anna cannot help experiencing a positive feeling toward him.

The point is that feelings come to us passively. The knowledge that John and Anna have so far does not reflect who their new acquaintances are. It may turn out that the Raiders fan is a nice person, while the watercolor painter is obnoxious. The feelings that John and Anna experience toward their new acquaintances do not imply that they are seeking their good. Feelings are not the same as true love. In order to understand this better, one has to be aware of two important principles.

PRINCIPLE I

Feelings Are Subjective

Feelings and sentiments are psychological situations (experiences) that happen inside of us. They are about how we feel, not about the good of others. We therefore say that feelings are subjective.

Feelings are good, but they are not true love. True love involves seeking the good of others—it involves the will.

PRINCIPLE II

When We Experience Strong Feelings, Our Perceptions of Reality Become Distorted

For example, when we feel angry we can lose contact with reality and say or do things that we later regret having said or done.

When a husband and wife argue, the conversation may get heated, and the wounds that they open with their words are sometimes difficult to heal. This can also happen to parents when they have to punish their children. At the end of the day, when parents are tired, the kids can get on their nerves. The dad—who is feeling angry—may lose his temper and end up yelling at his children. He probably does not want to do this, but the feeling of anger makes him say things that he will later regret.

The feeling that distorts our perception of reality can also be joy. During a soccer World Cup in the 90's there was a man in Rio de Janeiro who was watching one of Brazil's games. The TV was on the balcony of his condo, which was on the fifth or sixth floor, and he was sitting on a chair with his recently-born baby in his arms. It was an important game, things were getting tough, and Brazil needed to score. Finally Brazil scored, and the man was so enthused that he jumped up, raised his arms, and shouted "Goooooooooooal"—and in the process of raising his arms he threw the baby over the balcony without realizing what he had done. Only when his emotions calmed down did he ask himself, "Where is the baby?" He soon realized that his son was dead in the middle of the street, five or six floors below. This is a true story that appeared in the newspapers.

Although it is an extreme example, we have to be aware that when we experience strong feelings, we may easily lose contact with reality and do things that we later regret. The lesson to be learned is that we should not let our feelings and emotions rule our life.

2.2 *Eros*

We have seen that love is a single reality with two different dimensions. In the case of the love between a man and a woman, we will look at these dimensions by looking at the faculties that are involved.

1. *Sentimentality.* In the same way that a man may have an emotional attraction to a friend because he roots for the same football team, he may also experience an emotional attraction to a woman because of some trait of her personality, like her creativity, her compassion, her intuition, or her optimism. Likewise, a woman may also experience an emotional attraction to a man because of some trait of his personality, like his daring, the way he speaks, or his sense of humor.

2. *Sensuality.* Besides experiencing positive feelings toward a woman, a man may also find himself physically drawn to the beauty of her body. And a woman, besides experiencing positive feelings toward a man, may also find herself physically drawn to his body. This physical attraction comes from the sexual appetite.

3. *Will.* This is the faculty that prompts us to make the decision to seek the other person's good.

Sentimentality and sensuality combine to produce very powerful emotions and sentiments that shape how a man and a

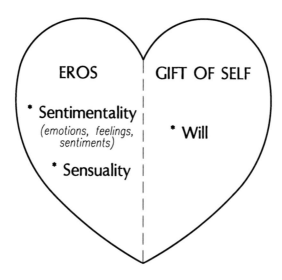

woman interact with each other. *Sensuality* is based on sexual pleasure and is attracted to the body, while *sentimentality* is attracted to the beloved as a person of the opposite sex (not just as a body of the opposite sex).

If a woman discovers that she feels good whenever a particular man is around, that she cannot avoid thinking about him during the day... then she is falling in love. This falling in love is an emotional situation that comes to her. Her feelings are fueled by physical attraction and have a component of sexual desire. This mixture of physical attraction, sexual desire, and intense feelings and emotions is called *eros* or erotic love. (The distinction between sensuality and sentimentality is only for the purpose of the discussion. In real situations, of course, both are intertwined with each other).

To fall in love is a feeling that comes to us and invades our emotional life. It is a feeling that is not planned nor willed, but rather that imposes itself on us. Feelings come to us passively, while true love comes from us actively.

Erotic love can enrich true love, but it is not true love, for it does not seek the good of the other. *Eros* is need-love; it is an experience caused by a sexual value that can provide the "raw material" for true love.[2]

We cannot separate erotic love from gift-love as we can separate the two slices of bread in a sandwich. Erotic love and gift-love are two dimensions of one single reality. What goes on between a man and a woman is true love only if the erotic dimension is raised to the level of gift-love.

Eros can only be raised to the level of gift-love if the man respects the dignity of the woman (the fact that she is an "I"), and the woman respects the dignity of the man (the fact that he is an "I"). In the following chapters we will look with more detail at what it means to respect the dignity of the person whom we love. We now apply to *eros* the two principles that were mentioned above.

PRINCIPLE I

Romantic Feelings Are Subjective

Romantic feelings are about "how I feel about her," they are about the subject who feels. Romantic feelings are subjective. They can help the development of true love, and they can enrich true love, but they are not true love.

PRINCIPLE II

When We Experience Strong Romantic Feelings, Our Perceptions of Reality Become Distorted

The distortion of reality that happens when one experiences strong feelings is especially intense in the case of erotic love. When someone falls in love, the feeling is so intense that it usually takes several months before one is able to see that the beloved is anything but perfect.

This is one of the reasons why we do crazy things when we fall in love, like starting to sing in the middle of the street, or writing letters that a few months later we are ashamed of. This also explains why some people who fall in love ignore their friends for months, or why most young people do not like to introduce their dates to their parents right away (at the beginning they are so blinded by their feelings, that they would not accept the slightest critical comment about their boyfriend or girlfriend—even if it is true).

True love requires us to exercise control over our feelings, which is an aspect of the virtue of temperance. It also requires us to seek the good of the other continuously, and this perseverance is part of the virtue of fortitude. It also demands generosity, the virtue by which we freely give to others what belongs to us. True love is not a feeling that comes to us; true love can only come from us if we have certain virtues. In the next chapter we will discuss what virtue is and how to acquire it.

Notes

[1] Because we cannot control the arising of our feelings, we are not directly responsible for them. However, once they have arisen in us, the will can approve the feelings, command them to flourish, or command them to cease. If the will participates (either actively promoting them or by mere consent), then we are responsible for our feelings. For example, you may feel angry because your neighbor is playing music too loud; this feeling is natural and you are not responsible for it. But if the intensity of your anger goes beyond what he deserves (say, if you internally desire his death), then you are responsible for that feeling. The same would apply if you willingly harbor that anger for months.

[2] As is obvious, erotic love can also provide the raw material for using the other person as an object.

CHAPTER 3

The Importance of Virtue

3.1 What Is Virtue?

An athlete may have the natural talent to win a gold medal, but if he does not train, he will not win it. Athletes are subject to a very demanding training schedule, so that their body can easily perform at a top level.

If you decide to play any sport, the first game of the season will make you tired. You then train, and the second game is easier. The third game will be easier still. This happens because your body gets used to higher levels of physical exercise. In the realm of our inner life, virtue is the equivalent of that ease in performing that training provides.

Habits are stable inclinations or dispositions to do something. Consider the habit of brushing your teeth before going to bed. As a child it is annoying, but then it becomes less difficult, until it takes no effort because it becomes something that we do automatically—it becomes second nature.

Virtue is a stable inclination or disposition to do good. Virtues are good habits. For example, the virtue of obedience is a stable inclination to obey; sincerity is a stable disposition to tell the truth; perseverance is a stable disposition to be constant in what we do (our studies, our work, or our marriage). All these virtues are difficult in the beginning, but with effort they become easier, like brushing our teeth.

Vice is a stable inclination or disposition to do evil. Examples include harming others, laziness, disorder, wasting time, teasing or picking on others, cheating, lying... If you do it once, and then again, and again, each time you become more inclined to do it again. If we get used to lying, it becomes a habit that is difficult to uproot.

If virtues are so important, how do we acquire them? It turns out that there is only one way, namely, by practice, by repetition of specific acts of the corresponding virtue. The only way for an athlete to get into shape is to train, one day after another. The same happens with virtue.

If you are disorderly and disorganized, the only way to become an orderly and tidy person is to practice. Keeping your desk and your closet in order, making your bed, keeping your books and notes in order, paying your bills on time, keeping your car tidy... today, and tomorrow, and the next day. It will be difficult in the beginning, but it becomes easier each day, until you do not even notice the effort. It becomes second nature, and you become an orderly person.

John has a strong character, but he has been struggling for years to control himself. Whenever he gives a rude answer he apologizes, and he tries to be polite at home and when others are around. Sometimes he still reacts abruptly, but there is a constant effort on his part and, as a consequence, month after month it becomes easier for him to control his bad temper. This is virtue. He has developed a stable inclination to be gentle and polite.

If you want to be sincere and always tell the truth, the only way to do so is by speaking the truth today, and tomorrow, and the day after. It may be difficult, but it is the only way to build a habit. If you are truthful now, next time you will have a stronger disposition to tell the truth. The same happens with bad habits.

It is important to emphasize that we acquire virtues by doing, not by thinking. An athlete cannot become accomplished just by thinking about his event; he needs to train. On a cold winter's day you cannot get warm by thinking about a good chimney fire; you need to get close to the fire. The same applies to virtues. You may know a lot about them, but if you do not practice, your knowledge will be useless.

3.2 Why is Virtue Important?

When you compare two quarterbacks, you can say that one is better than the other by the number of touchdowns, completions, and other statistics that measure performance. When you compare two pitchers, you can say that one is better than the other by their ERA, number of wins, etc. When you compare two students, you can say that one is better than the other (among other things) by their grades.

If you compare two people, how can you say that one is a better person than the other? This is a difficult question. What makes a person a better person is his virtues. (In practice, of course, it is difficult to compare because we do not "see" those virtues).

The reward for many touchdowns and completions is a big contract. The reward for being a good student is getting into a good college. The reward for virtue is being a better person; the reward for virtue is virtue itself. Note that all the other rewards are external (a big contract or going to a good college). In the case of virtue, however, its reward remains in us; we improve as persons.

If you would like to get married and raise a happy family, you will need many virtues. You may have the conditions, the talents, and the desire to be a good husband or a good wife. You may have the conditions of a great athlete. But if you do not train, you will not win the gold medal.

3.3   Three Basic Principles

Before moving on, we will discuss three basic principles that provide a background setting for what follows:

I. *All created things are good.* The fact that knives may be used for the wrong purpose (such as stabbing someone), does not mean that knives are bad. We can put things to bad use that in themselves are good.

II. *All things are created for a purpose.* If you do not agree with this principle, try to think of something that has been created for no purpose. There are many things that have been created for meaningless purposes, but here we are not talking about the quality of the purpose. An object may be used for a reason other than that for which it was created (a kitchen knife may be used to stab someone), but this does not contradict the fact that "everyone who makes anything makes it for some purpose."[1]

III. *All things are created with "rules of use."* What would happen if instead of detergent, you put ink in a washing machine? What would happen if instead of gas, you put coke in your car's tank? The following true story illustrates the point.

When microwave ovens first appeared, an older lady went to buy one. The next day she returned to the store to buy another one. The employee told her that if there was anything wrong with the first microwave, they would replace it with a new one. The lady insisted that she wanted to buy another microwave. The employee insisted that their goal was complete customer satisfaction, and that they would replace the original one. After a while the lady ended up acknowledging that the previous day, after buying the microwave, she took her little dog for a walk, it began raining, and the dog got wet. When she returned home she put the dog in the microwave in order to "dry it." Obviously, the little dog did not survive, and the microwave was rendered useless... so she wanted to buy another one. The point is that things are created with rules of use and, if we do not respect those rules, then they get broken or destroyed.

3.4 Fortitude

In the life of every person, two elements are always present: pleasure and pain (difficulties). The virtue of fortitude helps us deal with pain and difficulties. Fortitude is a permanent disposition to overcome or endure personal shortcomings, discomfort, physical pain, setbacks, or disappointments in order to achieve high goals.

Changing diapers is not fun. Parents do it, however, because they have a high goal. In order to raise their children, good parents endure all types of inconveniences with perseverance, even when they are tired or sick. Good parents are an example of how to develop the virtue of fortitude. First, they set high goals for themselves (raising a good family is a high goal). Second, they endure the difficulties that they meet on the way to achieving that goal.

In the same way that an athlete cannot win the gold medal by practicing just the week before the Olympics, we cannot acquire the endurance needed to achieve high goals by practicing just the day before. Virtue is not a one-time deal. In order to acquire any virtue we need to practice consistently over a prolonged period of time, and for this we need patience and perseverance.

Patience helps us endure suffering and difficulties until we achieve the good. Perseverance helps us to keep going until the goal is achieved. We say that these virtues are "parts" of fortitude.

True love requires us to give ourselves, and this is difficult. Without fortitude it is impossible.

3.5   Pleasure and the Appetites

The virtue that helps us deal with pleasure is temperance. Let us first look at why pleasure exists. Can man survive without eating or drinking? Can the human race survive without people marrying and having children? In the same way, science would not advance without curiosity, and society would not exist without justice being enforced.

Man has been endowed with some built-in tendencies to help him survive and develop as a human being. These tendencies are called *appetites,* like hunger, thirst, the sexual appetite, curiosity, or anger (in the sense of a tendency to avenge injustice, or to recover the use of our rights).

These appetites were designed to have pleasure associated with them. If we did not like to eat, we would starve and die; if we did not like to drink, we would dehydrate; if there were no pleasure associated with sex, men and women would not be very interested in each other and the human race would die out; if curiosity and anger did not provide any pleasure, science would not advance and we would not react against injustices (society would be chaotic, parents would not correct their children, and we would all be spoiled).

Pleasure and the appetites have been created for a purpose and with rules of use. For example, the purpose of the appetite of anger is to avenge injustice and to recover the use of our rights (although it can certainly be used for other purposes); the purpose of thirst is to hydrate our body; and so on with the rest of the appetites.

Temperance is equivalent to moderation or self-control. Temperance helps us bring the appetites into harmonious control, so that we respect their rules of use, as well as the purpose for which they were created. Besides the appetites, temperance also extends to the use of our time, to the desire for material goods, and to other enjoyable activities (like sports, hobbies, dancing, music, computer games, internet, watching TV, weight lifting, parties, etc.)

Temperance applied to the appetite of thirst is called sobriety. Temperance applied to the sexual appetite is called purity and chastity. Temperance applied to anger is called meekness and gentleness. Temperance applied to the possession and enjoyment of material goods is called detachment.

3.6   The "Automatic Mechanism"

The appetites are always within us, but they are not always active. The appetite of hunger is inactive most of the time; it is only when we go for a long time without food that hunger gets turned on and a desire for food is aroused in us. This strong desire is called a "passion." In the same way, the appetite of anger is not always active; if someone threatens your wife, the appetite of anger will arouse in you a passion for justice, and you will hasten to defend her.

A beautiful woman in a bikini is something attractive to any man and it generates an automatic response by the sexual appetite (a desire to look). This initial desire is automatic. After the initial prompting, the will has to decide whether to look or not.

If you go to the doctor early in the morning and he tells you that you should not eat solid food until the next morning, by the end of the day you will be hungry. If in the evening you pass by a restaurant and you see someone eating a hamburger, you will want to eat it—even though your reason tells you that you should not. When one is hungry the appetite of hunger gets turned on and all it wants is food, whatever it may be, and independent of whether it may damage your health or ruin your figure.

We say that the appetite of hunger is blind, in the sense that it is not attracted specifically to a chicken sandwich, or to a bowl of pasta. It is attracted to food. Any kind of food that is pleasing to us will do.

An analogous thing happens with the rest of the appetites. When we are really thirsty we do not care whether it is coke, lemonade, or water; we just want to quench our thirst. In the same way, the sexual appetite is awakened by any attractive member of the opposite sex.[2] This initial attraction is not wrong in itself, for *eros* is attracted mainly to the body. Any attractive body of the opposite sex can turn on the sexual appetite. We say that *eros* is blind. True love, however, is not blind, for it involves the decision of the will to seek the good of the other.

We all know that vice is easy, while virtue is difficult. We all experience that we do not have perfect control over the appetites. For example, even though our reason might tell us that we should not look at the woman in a bikini, the appetite may still win due to its strong inclination to en-

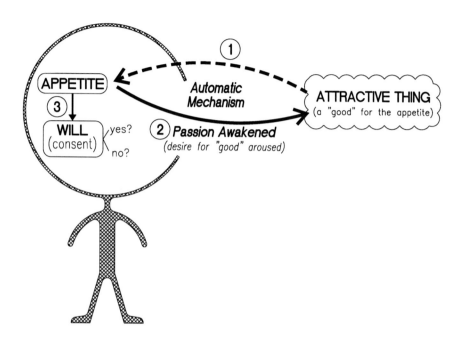

joy pleasure without moderation. This inclination is called concupiscence.[3] In the picture above, the downward arrow marked with the number 3 represents the strong influence that the appetites can exert on the will.

In order to have control over the appetites, we ought to strengthen our will with virtue. In particular, temperance will give us an inclination to respect the purpose of the appetites and their rules of use. This is a very important element of character.

People without temperance always do what "feels good." If you want to be a person with character, you need temperance in order to have control over yourself. People with temperance have control over the appetites and are masters of themselves.

There is a widespread notion today that love is a feeling, and that the more intense the feeling, the deeper the love is. This is the message that Hollywood continuously sends through movies and television. Many people think that following one's feelings is the way to express love. But true love is not about oneself, it is about the other. In the following chapters it will become clear that without virtue there can be no true love.

Notes

[1] Aristotle, *Ethics* (London: Penguin, 1976), p. 205 [1139b].

[2] We are only concerned here with normal situations. The particularities associated with same-sex attraction are beyond the scope of this book.

[3] Concupiscence is a disordered desire. Greed is the concupiscence of the eyes, a disordered attraction to the glittering of wealth and comfort, and to covet what others have. Pride is the concupiscence of one's ego, a disordered desire for personal glory, fame, or power. Lust is the concupiscence of the flesh, a disordered desire to enjoy sexual pleasure.

CHAPTER **4**

Love and the Gift of Self

In Chapter 2 we looked at *eros,* which is the subjective dimension of the love between a man and a woman. In this chapter we will study the other dimension, which is gift-love. The purpose of this chapter is to better understand what it means to give oneself completely.

4.1 Who Is Man?

When I have something, the recipient of the action is always "me." When I give something, the recipient is always someone else. Having is egocentric, while giving is centered on the other. (Egocentric is not the same as egotistic. Egocentric just means "centered on oneself"). The key is to find out what is more important, whether to have or to give.

In order to understand why the answer to this question is important, think of a caveman who goes out for a walk in the woods and happens to find a razor. Do you think he would use it to shave? At the beginning he would be perplexed by such a strange object. Then, after discovering

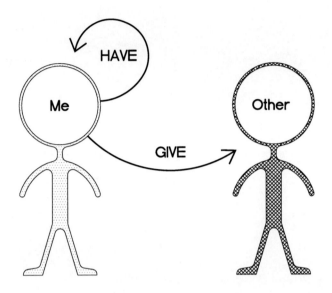

that it has a sharp edge, he might use the razor to cut wood or sharpen sticks, but he would not use it for the purpose for which it was created. As a consequence, the razor will get dented. This example shows that an incorrect notion of what things are leads to their wrong use, and they get damaged.

In an analogous way, an incorrect notion of what a person is leads to behaviors that make the person unable to achieve happiness. How we live largely depends on the concept that we have of what a person is.

The following argument will help us understand that man is made for "giving," that the full development of the person is achieved through the complete gift of one's self.

Think of a sculptor who takes a block of marble and gives it a beautiful shape. Does the marble have anything that the sculptor did not give it? The shape is certainly a gift from the sculptor, but the marble's existence is its own. The marble was already there before receiving the shape.

With this example in the background, we can now ask ourselves whether we have anything that God did not give us. The answer is subtle because when we were created we also received some gifts, but not like the block of marble. The marble was already there and it received the shape as a gift. We, however, were not here before being created, so there is no receiver of the gift which is distinct from the gift itself. We may then say that everything that we have, including our own existence, comes from God.

But there is a little catch to this argument, for one of the gifts that we received is freedom. If we are forced to give something, then we cannot call it a gift; a gift is something that we freely give to others. What we give is something that even God cannot do for us. What we give to others is in fact the only thing that we can truly call our own—the rest is either a gift that we have received, or something that we have acquired using those God-given talents.[1] At the end of our lives we will only *have* what we *gave* (with rectitude of intention).

There is a law engraved in the heart of every man, namely, that "one should do good and avoid evil." Two people may not agree as to what good and evil are in a specific situation, but everyone agrees that to do good and avoid evil is an obvious law of human behavior.[2] It is in this sense that man finds within himself a longing to do good, a yearning to achieve excellence and to live in such a way that he may "have" something when his life comes to an end. Because at the end of his life man will only be able to claim as his what he gave to others, we say that man finds within himself a desire to give.

As the highest degree of giving consists of giving one's own self, man finds within his heart a desire to give himself completely.

4.2 Friendship

Friendship is initially based on something about your friend that you like or enjoy—it is initially based on need-love. You may be interested in a friend because he has free tickets to the football games, or because he has a sister that you like. So far it is only need-love (it is only about you). There is nothing wrong with this, but if you do not seek his good, you would be using him as a means to your own ends.

If you think about your friend only because of the free tickets, but you do not even call him when he has a broken arm, then you are treating him more as an object than as a person. If your neighbor has a great lawn mower and that is the only reason why you are interested in being friends with him, you are using him as a means to your own ends. True friendship would require you to be genuinely interested in him, and not only in his lawn mower.

When friendship remains at the level of need-love, it can be very selfish. "Need-love friends" (buddies) are usually ego-centric relationships. Having a lot of buddies is just having; it does not involve giving.

For true friendship to exist, we need to give ourselves. We can give free tickets to football games to our friends, or we can give them our time, such as when we teach them how to play the guitar, or when we give them a ride. We can also share with them ideas, emotions, feelings, loves, fears, or details about our family that we would not mention to strangers.

When we share personal things with a friend and he shares personal things with us, there is a sort of unification of the "I"s. His "I" becomes as it were my own, and my "I" becomes his own.

When there is true friendship, it is easy to give advice to our friends and to receive advice from them. Giving advice to a friend is a way of seeking his good. If you realize that your friend Joe always arrives late and you let him know in a kind way, you are seeking his good (if you do not tell him, he might get fired from his job). At the same time, we expect our friends to point out our defects frankly, and to console us in times of sorrow or trial.

Love in friendship is not a sensual love, for it seeks primarily the good of the other, not the good of oneself. Gift-love does not suppress our need-loves; you still enjoy going to the football games for free with Joe, or borrowing his lawn mower, but you are not interested in him only because of that. You are interested in him because you feel his "I" as your "I", and his concerns as your concerns. This is true friendship (assuming there is reciprocity).

4.3   Giving Oneself Completely

In friendship each person seeks the good of the other, but there is a special type of love where each person gives himself completely to the other. We call it betrothed love.

> The essence of betrothed love is self-giving, the surrender of one's "I". This is something different from and more than attraction, desire or even goodwill. These are all ways by which one person goes out towards another, but none of them can take him as far in his quest for the good of the other as does betrothed love...The fullest, the most uncompromising form of love consists precisely in self-giving, in making one's inalienable and non-transferable "I" someone else's property.[3]

The notion of the complete gift of one's self poses a very difficult question, namely, how can I give my own "I"? How

can I make my "I" someone else's property? We can own a
house, a car, or a cow, but we cannot own a person. The key
element of our inner life is freedom; being a person implies
being one's own master. So what does it mean to give oneself
completely? Does the person need to give up being his own
master?

Even if we wanted to give our inner life away, we could
not do it because a person is untransferable or incommunicable. We can transfer a kidney from one body to another,
but we cannot transfer inner life from one body to another.
Our inner life always remains ours; it is precisely what defines who we are. The nature of the person is incompatible
with giving itself away.

You can buy a car and transfer its property from the
seller to yourself. However, that which is personal (the world
of emotions, desires, loves, affections, and longings that define our subjectivity) is on a plane where there can be no
transfer or appropriation in the physical sense, as if the person were an object. Nevertheless,

> What is impossible and illegitimate in the natural
> order and in a physical sense, can come about in
> the order of love and in a moral sense. In this sense,
> one person can give himself or herself, can surrender
> completely to another, whether to a human person
> or to God, and such a giving of the self creates a spe-
> cial form of love which we define as betrothed love.[4]

When a man gives himself completely to a woman, he gives
her his time, his affections, his desires, his thoughts, his eyes,
and all that he has. A man cannot give himself completely
to two women because, if he gives everything to one, then
he has nothing left for the other. The complete gift of self
requires *exclusivity*.

Suppose that Vince tells Kim, "I'll give myself to you for three years, but after that... we'll see." Or, "I'll give myself to you for as long as you look as gorgeous as you look now; after that, I reserve the right to find another woman." This obviously is not complete self-giving. Besides exclusivity, the complete gift of self also requires *permanence*.

The notion of completeness is one of the key concepts of this book, and the reader will get more out of it if he spends a few minutes considering on his own how exclusivity and permanence are requirements of completeness. When the exclusive and permanent gift is mutual, we call it marriage.[5]

> Marriage is the exclusive and permanent gift
> of self between a man and a woman.

The key to the inner life that defines who we are is freedom. Giving oneself completely means giving one's freedom to another being. This has to be properly understood because we have seen that the person is not transferable. I cannot transfer my freedom to another person in the physical sense. However, I can freely choose to limit my freedom in order to unite my will to another person's will.

This limitation of one's freedom reaches its highest degree when it is exclusive and permanent. When this happens, we say that the person gives himself completely.

The fact that a *complete* gift is defined by a limitation may seem to be a contradiction. This apparent contradiction, however, stems from our tendency to think in physical terms. If we completely empty a glass of water, no water at all is left in the glass. In an analogous way, when we say that we give ourselves completely, we tend to think that no

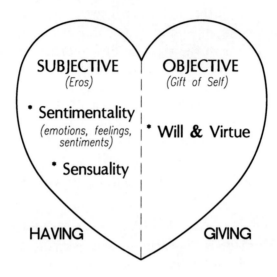

freedom at all should remain in us. But this cannot happen because our freedom is always ours, it is part of who we are. The complete gift of one's self means that the limitation of our freedom on behalf of the other person should reach the highest degree compatible with being who we are. This happens when such limitation is exclusive and permanent.

The key of the gift of self is not the negative aspect of limiting our freedom, but rather the positive one of uniting our will with the will of the beloved. "I surrender my freedom to you because I want to live exclusively and permanently for you." When we give ourselves, our "I" is not limited or shrunk, but rather it is enlarged and enriched. When we give ourselves we find a fuller existence in the other person (or with the other person). When he gives up the football game in order to go shopping with his wife, Vince does not see it as sacrifice because he finds his happiness in being with her.

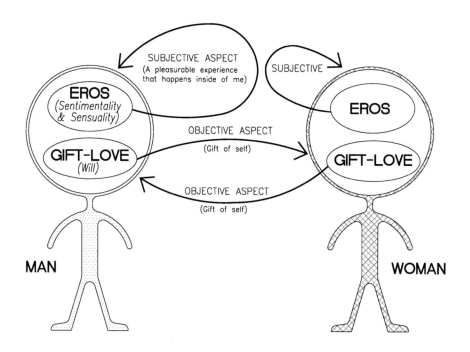

As we cannot give something that we do not have, it follows that if we do not have ourselves, then we will not be able to give ourselves. "Having oneself" means being master of oneself. This is why lack of self-control represents such a threat to our development as persons. Without self-control we cannot possess ourselves, so we cannot give ourselves. Lack of self-control means that true love cannot develop. Without virtue there can be no true love.

What we have learned so far can be summarized in the figures on the preceding page and on this page, where "objective" means that gift-love is centered on the other person, who is the "object" of our love.

Notes

[1] This is analogous to what happens in a company when you develop a patent. Although you came up with the idea, the patent belongs to the company because you developed it with the resources, funding, and talent that the company made available to you.

[2] If the good is "that at which all things aim," then everyone should want to avoid evil, which is the opposite of good. See Aristotle, *Ethics* (London: Penguin, 1976), p. 63 [1094a].

[3] K. Wojtyla, *Love and Responsibility* (San Francisco: Ignatius, 1993), pp. 96-97.

[4] K. Wojtyla, *Love and Responsibility* (San Francisco: Ignatius, 1993), pp. 96-97.

[5] A person can also give himself exclusively to God. Such is the case, for example, of a priest, a religious, a numerary or associate member of Opus Dei, or a celibate member of an ecclesial movement. This is called "apostolic celibacy," and it also entails exclusivity and permanence.

CHAPTER **5**

Love and the Nuptial Meaning of the Body

5.1   The Language of the Body

Man is unique and unrepeatable above all, but not exclusively, because of his inner life. If the only reason for man's uniqueness were his inner life, the body would be like an external instrument—like a belt, a shirt, or a racquet.

In order to do something as simple as expressing our ideas, we need a special type of body (if we had a cow's body, we could neither write nor talk). In order to express the richness of our inner life we need a human body; the body has a good part in shaping who we are.

In particular, masculinity or femininity are an important dimension of who we are. In the case of animals, sexuality is an instinct that is exclusively at the service of procreation. When a male dog and a female dog mate, their sexual union is just a union of bodies; there is nothing more to it. Man's sexuality, however, is something more than sexual instinct because man can refer to himself as an "I".

The human body is the expression of a person's "I". This means that every conscious action of a person is an expression of his inner life, an expression of who he is. For example, snoring while asleep does not express any aspect of one's inner life because it is not a conscious act. However, the way a person laughs is an expression of his inner life; the way he eats a hamburger is an expression of who he is; giving alms is an expression of who the person is; sexual intercourse is also an expression of who the person is.

A person's sexual activity is not just sexual instinct (as it is in the case of animals). The sexual union of dogs is a purely animal act; it is a union of two bodies. The sexual union of a man and a woman is not an animal act; it is a personal act, an act that involves two "I"s.

We have seen that, besides the language of words, there is also a language of the body. This language is made up of the way we talk, the way we act, the way we laugh, the way we dress, the way we walk, the way we dance, and so on.

For example, to shake hands with a friend is a physical expression of respect. To give your father a big hug is an external manifestation of love for your father. To kiss your spouse when you leave the house is a physical expression of love for your spouse. All these signs are different ways of showing, with your body, the love that you have for others.

You shake hands with a new customer, but you do not kiss him. If the mailman delivers a letter or a package to your home, you thank him, but you do not embrace him. If you go to a see a professor during office hours, you greet him upon entering his office, but you do not wrap your arm around his waist. The day you leave for college you do not limit yourself to shaking hands with your parents; you give them a big hug.

A young man may say, "As I love my girlfriend, I express my love by having sex with her." This man, however, also loves his mother and his sisters, but hopefully he does not express this love by having sexual relations with them. (Likewise, a young woman loves her father and her brothers, but hopefully she does not have sexual relations with them). The point is that different external expressions of love have different meanings. A kiss, a hug, shaking hands, and sexual intercourse are external signs of love, but they have different meanings.

From a physical point of view, sexual intercourse expresses completeness, in the sense that *physically* there is nothing left to be given. Other signs (like a kiss, a hug, an embrace, or holding hands) can also express love, but none of them expresses completeness.

To lie is to say something that is not true, something that does not fit reality. For instance, the statement "San Diego lies in the Northeast of the United States" is false because it does not fit reality. Likewise, the statement "Snow is black" is false because it does not fit reality. Truth is the correspondence of our intelligence to reality.

In an analogous way, when the language of the body does not fit reality, we also lie. Brian is angry with his mother because she grounded him. The next day Brian wants to hang out with his friends, and he needs permission and cash. Even though he is still upset with her, Brian puts on a smile and, with the sole intention of obtaining permission and money, he kisses her goodnight. This kiss is not sincere, for he is still upset with his mother. His action (the kiss) does not fit the reality of his inner life. His kiss is a lie.

In the same way, if the language of the body expresses completeness, but the man and the woman do not give themselves completely, the sexual union is a lie. In other words, if there is a union of bodies without an exclusive and permanent commitment between the man and the woman, the sexual union is a lie.

Something that happens frequently to young men and women who are not careful in selecting their dates is that, after a romantic evening, one suggests, "Why don't we make love?" The young man or woman initially says no. The other one insists, "If you really loved me, you would have sex with me." If the young man or the young woman does not want to lose the other one, he or she ends up giving in. Then they begin to wonder what is wrong with having sexual intercourse. "If we love each other so much, why shouldn't we express our love in that way?"

This reasoning contains an error. While their union expresses completeness physically, such union of bodies does not represent a complete union of persons. If it did, then his time, his thoughts, his affections, and his everything would belong to her, and she would belong to him (which is what we call marriage). Without an exclusive and permanent commitment, their sexual union would be a lie.

Gabe and Marga have been dating for several years. One day he proposes to her, she accepts, and they fix a wedding date. As they are already engaged, they start having sex. In this case the commitment is exclusive, but not permanent. Being only engaged, they can walk away at any moment, so there is no union of persons.

The same happens with contraceptives. If husband and wife were to use contraceptives, the language of the body during sexual intercourse would express completeness, but they would not be giving themselves completely. They would be keeping for themselves their fertility, which is part of who they are. The use of contraceptives in marriage is also a very deep lie.

If a man were to tell his wife, "Honey, I don't like your hair, so I am going to wrap a bag around your head while we make love," then he would not be interested in her, but only in a part of her body. He would be using his wife as an instrument for sexual gratification. This is precisely what happens with contraceptives, for the spouses are leaving out part of the "I" (their fertility).

After all this, a person may say, "I agree that sex before marriage is a lie. In fact, when I have sex with my girlfriend I realize that something is missing, but... it is such a pleasurable lie that I don't care about lying a little bit. And my girlfriend doesn't care either." What is wrong with this?

First, when we lie to someone, we are not respecting his dignity. And we have seen that when the dignity of the other person is not respected, the relationship cannot be true love (we would be using the other person as an object).

Second, one of the foundations of marriage is trust. Sex before marriage undermines trust because it is a lie. And without trust, true love cannot exist. One of the reasons that explains the high divorce rate is the widespread sexual activity before marriage.[1]

Third, when we do not follow the "rules of use" that were created for our own good, we damage ourselves. One of these rules is to speak the truth and avoid lying. Sex before marriage (as well as sex in marriage with contraceptives) is a lie that damages one's own self in a very deep way.[2]

Fourth, for the person who believes in God, lying is a sin and it offends God.[3]

5.2   The Nuptial Meaning of the Body

We have seen that our actions have the capacity to express different aspects of our inner life. As sexual intercourse expresses completeness physically, it has the capacity to become an outward sign of the complete gift of the persons. Because this complete gift is what we call marriage, we say that the body has a matrimonial or nuptial meaning.

The nuptial meaning of the body is its capacity to express, in a physical way, the completeness of the inner gift of self. It shows that the attraction of the bodies exists in us to stimulate the union of the persons. This sexual attraction of man to femininity and of woman to masculinity is not the same as lust (which is disordered sexual desire).

In the case of animals, the attraction of the bodies only exists for the purpose of procreation. Sexual intercourse between animals has no personal meaning because there is no "I" to be given. In human beings, the permanent attraction of men to what is feminine, and of women to what is masculine, is a physical expression of the desire to give ourselves completely that we find in our hearts.

Vince and Kim have been married for a few years and have three children. One day Kim gets ill and the doctor tells her that, if she gets pregnant again, there might be a serious risk for her life. Kim and Vince talk about it and decide to use contraceptives, or that Kim gets a tubal ligation.[4] Is such a decision justified in this case?

Vince seems to be saying, "If you get pregnant, there might be a serious risk for your health. Because I love you and I don't want you to die, I think we should use contraceptives." Does it make sense in this case?

If they use contraceptives, Vince and Kim would be leaving out not only their fertility, but also Kim's medical condition (which is an element of who she is). If they use contraceptives, the gift of self would not be complete, and the lack of correspondence between the language of the body and the reality of who they are would be a lie.[5]

When one aspect of the dignity of the human being is denied, the person ends up being used as an object. If fertility is left out, the couple is disregarding one aspect of who the person is, and the door is then open to disregarding other aspects. For example, if the wife is involved in a serious car accident and her face is disfigured, the same principle that justifies the use of contraceptives (disrespect for one aspect of who she is) would justify the husband to leave his wife in order to find a more attractive woman; he would just be disregarding another aspect of who she is (her appearance).

If the husband falls into a severe depression, leaving him in order to find a man with a more attractive personality would mean disregarding another aspect of who he is. Once an aspect is left out, disregarding another one is no big deal. This does not mean that all couples who use contraceptives or who had sex before getting married end up in divorce. It means that if the gift is not complete, there cannot be true love, even if the couple stays together.

Suppose now that Vince and Kim decide not to use contraceptives, but rather to limit sexual relations to the periods when Kim is not fertile and, therefore, cannot get pregnant. This recourse to periodic continence is called Natural Family Planning, or NFP. (Details are discussed in the Appendix). Does this respect the dignity of the person?

Part of who a woman is, is her periodic fertility (the monthly cycle of fertility is controlled by several hormones that also produce changes in her inner moods). Limiting sexual intercourse to the times when the woman is not fertile is therefore respectful of the dignity of the body.

Think of a young couple who are both healthy and have no financial problems. They realize that if they have (more) children they will not be able to buy a nice house in the best part of town, and they will not be able to have expensive cars, nor take vacations to fancy destinations. At the same time, they realize that using contraceptives does not respect the dignity of the person, so in order to avoid children they decide to limit sexual relations to the times of the month when she is infertile. Their actions respect the dignity of the body. Do they respect the dignity of the person?

Consider the following example. While giving alms is a good action, a person may decide to make a large donation to his church in order to impress the pastor, or just to show off and let everybody know how much money he has. This example illustrates how a bad intention can ruin an action that, in itself, is good.

This is also what happens to the young couple. They do not use contraceptives, but their intention (to hold back their fertility) ruins an action that otherwise would be good. They use NFP with a contraceptive mentality.

Let us go back to the case when Kim could die if she got pregnant. Vince may say something like, "If you get pregnant again, there might be a serious risk for your health. As I love you, I think you should not get pregnant. At the same time, because I want to respect who you are (which includes your illness and your fertility), we can limit sexual intercourse to the times when you are not fertile." When they do so, their intention is not to leave fertility out, but to avoid the potential fatal consequences for Kim's life.

In the case of the healthy couple with no financial problems, their intention is to leave fertility out (the gift of self, therefore, would not be complete). Note how the intention makes such a big difference, and how NFP methods can be used with a contraceptive mentality.

Besides risk for the woman's life, there are other reasons that could make it appropriate for a couple to limit sexual relations to the periods when the woman is infertile. Think for example, of a woman who is in good physical condition but, after having two children, she sees that the kids get on her nerves and gets stressed out and exhausted.

Spouses have to decide with generosity whether their reasons for spacing births are well-grounded, knowing that the truth of their love is at stake.

5.3 Temperance and the Nuptial Meaning of the Body

Chastity, which is part of the virtue of temperance, helps us use our sexuality following the "rules of use" that were designed for our own good. It regulates voluntary expressions of sexual pleasure in marriage, and excludes them altogether outside marriage.

Purity, which is also part of the virtue of temperance, is somewhat broader. Purity moves a person to abstain from actions, thoughts, ways of dressing, dancing, speaking, or looking that are likely to arouse unlawfully the sexual appetite in oneself or in others. When a woman dresses immodestly, she is likely to arouse the sexual appetite in others; if you talk about dirty stuff, you may arouse the sexual appetite in yourself and in others; if you listen to songs with bad lyrics, your sexual appetite may also be aroused.

The following example illustrates how the way we look is deeply related with our love.[6] Vince and his wife Kim go out for a walk and a young attractive woman passes by, walking toward them. When the young woman gets close, Vince begins to explore her curves and turns his head to follow her with his eyes... How do you think Kim will feel?

Vince is being unfaithful to Kim because, the day they married, he committed to live exclusively for her, while his behavior shows that he is not giving his eyes to her in an exclusive way. True love can only exist when every aspect of one's life is raised to the level of the complete gift of self. This includes our eyes and the way we look. It also includes our thoughts and imaginations.

If Vince spends time thinking about another woman, imagining that he is having sex with her, he would be keeping his thoughts and desires for himself. His wife would not be aware of it, but this does not matter. He would be keeping for himself something he had promised to give her. This is not complete self-giving and, therefore, it would not be compatible with true love.

Assume that Vince does not look at the other woman, but rather turns to Kim and, looking at her in the eyes, says, "Honey, I love you." With his actions, Vince is saying that Kim is number one. Kim would probably think, "Vince has not looked at that woman just for me; his actions show that he really loves me."

When the body is desired (whether with our eyes or in our thoughts) outside the context of the union of the whole person, we are taking something that should only exist at the level of the gift. Therefore, the need that we have written in our hearts to give ourselves completely is damaged. The person who looks lustfully at others, the one who looks at pornography, or the one who lets his thoughts and imagination go wild, is damaging his own self.[7]

Lust is disordered sexual desire. Even married people can treat themselves lustfully. A man who lets his imagination go wild with his wife is also damaging his own self, as is a woman who lets her thoughts go wild with her husband. These sexual phantasies would not be an expression of the complete gift of self, but rather a way of using the other person, even if only in one's thoughts.

To live chastity in marriage means to use sex according to the dignity of the person. The expression *conjugal chastity* refers to the use of sex only with one's spouse and without contraceptives (and using periodic continence only when there are well-grounded reasons to do so).

When the spouses give themselves, part of the gift is their fertility. Husband and wife have sexual relations whenever they please and they accept the number of children that may come, provided they can properly raise them.[8]

If there are well-grounded reasons to avoid having (more) children, the couple may have recourse to NFP methods in order to space births. This requires a good deal of self-mastery, for such methods require the spouses to avoid intercourse during a portion of each month. (See the Appendix for more details). This can be hard because they may have acquired a habit of having sexual relations with greater frequency. The spouses will need temperance and fortitude to persevere in their efforts to respect each other's dignity.

While the sexual drive in men is quite stable, women's sexual drive tends to vary with their hormonal cycle. And it happens that women usually experience the greatest sexual desire during ovulation, which is precisely when they are fertile and when the couple should avoid intercourse if they are using NFP methods. This makes it even harder for the woman to abstain during the fertile time of the cycle.

Virtue requires saying no to oneself. However, this renunciation is not an end in itself, but rather a means of gaining mastery over oneself so that one can give himself completely. The end goal of continence is not the negative aspect of avoiding intercourse (and babies); the end goal is to have mastery over oneself so that one becomes able to express true love, ensuring that the gift of the person is complete.

The nuptial meaning of the body is its capacity to express the complete gift of one's self, but this meaning is not exclusively limited to the sexual organs. Husband and wife can also express the inner gift of themselves with their body in ways that are not sexual. While the sexual union should always be an expression of the inner gift of self, the gift of self is not exclusively expressed by means of the sexual union. It is expressed by means of sexual intercourse in some circumstances, but it ought to be continuously expressed through a variety of daily manifestations of affection.

In terms of the framework that has been developed in previous chapters, this can be explained as follows. We have seen that erotic love is configured by sensuality and sentimentality. The first element (sensuality) is based on sexual pleasure and it tends to the sexual union; sensuality is attracted to the body. The second element (sentimentality) is also based on the fact that the other spouse is a member of the opposite sex, but it does not tend necessarily to sexual intercourse; sentimentality is attracted to the other spouse as a person (as a person of the opposite sex, certainly, but not just as a body of the opposite sex). Continence means that, during some periods, husband and wife work more on the emotional aspect of their love (sentimentality), which in this way develops and grows deeper. This obviously requires self-dominion in order to keep sensuality under control.

Periodic continence allows couples to discover the deeper aspects of the nuptial meaning of the body. Every couple who has used NFP has discovered how the self-imposed limitation to avoid intercourse during some periods forces the spouses to be more creative in finding ways of expressing their love. This creativity allows husband and wife to discover a greater meaning in small details of affection, like a simple kiss, a caress, or a hug—a meaning that beforehand was perhaps unknown to them, and that afterwards will give a greater richness to their intimate life. The nuptial meaning of the body is its capacity to express true love, but this nuptial meaning is not reduced to sexual meaning.[9]

Those who practice temperance in little things find it easier to live continence. Virtue opens up for the spouses the freedom of the gift—the capacity to give themselves completely. Those who want to give themselves completely should make a point of practicing daily in the different areas of temperance, like eating and drinking with moderation, controlling their reactions of anger, guarding their eyes and their imagination, controlling their curiosity, and making sure that they live detached from material goods.

Couples who have lived purity and chastity while dating realize that it is relatively easy for them to live periodic continence. They already have the habit of truly loving each other and, as this habit has become second nature, it is natural for them to respect the dignity of one another. The divorce rate among couples who use NFP is virtually zero.

This is easy to understand because the efforts to develop temperance makes it easier for the couple to live continence. At the same time, continence strengthens their temperance, which allows them to control their desires of self-affirmation. By strengthening temperance, continence frees spouses from their whims in their daily relationship, so that it is easier for them to control their tendency to selfishness.

Self-mastery is the door that gives access to the joy of true love. Externally, true love may seem to demand a lot of renunciation, and it may even appear as something negative, but it is only through this path of self-mastery that one can acquire the freedom to give oneself completely. A person who does not have control over himself will never experience true love, even if there is a wealth of positive emotions and feelings in the relationship with his spouse.

> There are two men, both of whom have a number of casks; the one man has his casks sound and full, one of wine, another of honey, and a third of milk, besides others filled with other liquids, and the streams which fill them are few and scanty, and he can only obtain them with a great deal of toil and difficulty; but when his casks are once filled he has no need to feed them any more, and has no further trouble with them or care about them. The other, in like manner, can procure streams though not without difficulty;

> but his vessels are leaky and unsound, and night
> and day he is compelled to be filling them, and if he
> pauses for a moment, he is in an agony of pain.[10]

Those who are not temperate have their jars full of holes.
They fill them with pleasure, but they always need more.
If they pause for a moment (say, if they need to abstain
from sexual relations for a few days), they are "in an agony
of pain." They do not know how to handle it because they
do not have enough virtue to control themselves. They need
more and more fleeting pleasures because they have not experienced the joy of true love.

Many marriages end in separation or divorce because,
due to their previous choices in life, the spouses cannot give
themselves completely. They can give their bodies, but they
lack the virtue to give their selves.

Notes

[1] Remaining a virgin until marriage does not guarantee that
the couple will not divorce, but it guarantees that the dignity of
the person is being respected, which is one of the conditions to
ensure that true love can exist.

[2] In Section 7.4 it is explained how one's self is damaged.

[3] Sex outside of marriage constitutes a lack of respect for human dignity because of the deep lie that is involved. Christ called
the devil "the father of all lies." Sex before marriage is a grave
sin because it is a deep lie.

[4] Contraceptives can roughly be grouped in three categories:
Barrier methods, like condoms or diaphragms; *Chemical contra-
ceptives,* like the pill, the contraceptive patch, the Intra-Uterine-
Device (IUD), implants (Norplant), hormone injections (Depro-
Provera), or spermicide gels; *Sterilization procedures,* which are
like permanent contraceptives (in a "tubal ligation," the woman's

fallopian tubes are closed, preventing the egg from travelling to the uterus from the ovary; in a "vasectomy," the conducts that carry the man's sperm are cut, preventing the sperm from mixing into the semen). Although other methods like onanism (spilling the semen outside the woman's body) do not fit in them, these three categories cover the most frequently used contraceptives.

[5] If Kim were to get on the pill without telling Vince (or if she were to get an IUD or a tubal ligation without Vince's knowledge, or with his opposition to it), then Vince would be giving himself completely, while Kim would be lying to her husband. If Vince were to get a vasectomy without telling his wife (or with her opposition to it), then Kim would be giving herself completely, while Vince would be lying to his wife.

[6] The example is adapted from J.R. Waiss, *Couples in Love* (New York: Crossroad, 2003), pp. 31-32.

[7] "While love involves sacrifice and commitment, pornography teaches you to reduce others to sexual objects that can be used and then discarded once your passion wears off... Pornography is the perfect way to ruin your future marriage. It trains the brain to be aroused by dirty, illicit, sexual fantasies. And, even though it takes only a few seconds to see the pictures, it takes years to forget them. This causes tremendous strain in marriage, because the spouse is compared to the models and is expected to provide as much excitement. When this does not happen, the couple suffers and the spouse feels hurt and unable to 'live up' to the fantasies. Who wants to put his or her future bride or groom through this?" See J. Evert, *Pure Love* (San Diego: Catholic Answers, 2003), pp. 16-17.

[8] True love requires generosity, which usually translates into large families. There are exceptions, like couples who cannot have children, or who can only have one or two, but when a man and a woman decide to give themselves completely, the normal (average) thing is to have a large family.

[9] "Conjugal chastity... is manifested at first as the capacity to resist the concupiscence of the flesh. It later gradually reveals

itself as a singular capacity to perceive, love and practice those
meanings of the language of the body which remain altogether
unknown to concupiscence itself. Those meanings progressively
enrich the marital dialogue of the couple, purifying it, deep-
ening it, and at the same time simplifying it. Therefore, [the]
asceticism of continence... does not impoverish affective manifestations. But rather it makes them spiritually more intense
and therefore enriches them." See John Paul II, *The Theology
of the Body* (Boston: Pauline, 1997), p. 409 [Oct. 24, 1984]. As
this work is a collection of weekly speeches, the speech's date is
provided in brackets.

[10] Plato, *Gorgias* (New York: Prometheus, 1996), 493.

CHAPTER 6

Love and Thinking of Others

6.1 Forgetting about Self

The life of a toddler is centered around himself. If a toddler does not get what he wants, he cries until he gets it. This is the only mechanism he has to survive (if a hungry toddler did not cry, he would not get fed). An eleven-year-old boy is usually concerned with having fun and getting more gadgets. His life is still centered around "me, me, me."

Think now of a good mother. She spends most of her time thinking about her children and her husband; how to save money here and there so that more is available to them; how to help the children with their school projects; what she can prepare for dinner that they will like; and so on. Children think mainly about themselves, while responsible adults think mainly about others.

In accordance with this description, teenagers are in the middle, in transition. A teenager ought to evolve from thinking mainly about himself to thinking of others. If a teenager does not learn to think of others during his teen years, it is likely that he will never learn.

Teenagers are usually concerned with their image (how they look, if they are attractive, if they are tall, if members of the opposite sex look at them). If you are a teenager and you want to become a mature adult, you have to learn to be less concerned about yourself, about your own image, about what others think of you, and be more concerned about others.

Once the teen years are gone, other concerns should absorb your energies, and you will live with the habits you have developed during your youth. Say that you have an exciting plan for the weekend, but your parents ground you. How would you feel? Well, this happens all the time in married life; you have an interesting plan, and then your spouse wants to do something else. If you do not have the habit of thinking of others, marriage will be a source of quarrels, and your marriage will suffer.

There are people who can take care of themselves, but are very immature. They have a job, make their own money, cook their own meals, do their own laundry... they take care of themselves, but they seldom care about others. Maturity is linked to the gift of self. People do not mature when they can take care of themselves; they mature when they can take care of others, and want to do so.[1]

If you want to be able to give yourself completely one day, you need to develop the habit of forgetting about yourself and thinking of others. A habit that is most important in this respect is that of serving others. In order to serve, it is necessary to seek the others' good, and this lies at the core of maturity.

- Do not wait until people ask you for help. Take the initiative. If no one at home has had time to do the dishes, take the initiative and wash them. If you are having dinner and someone needs napkins (or salad dressing, or a fork), instead of waiting to see who will get up, get up yourself and bring the napkins.

- If there is chicken for dinner and others like the wings, let them choose first. (Mothers are experts in this).

- Once you are done with your chores, offer to help others with theirs (if possible, in such a way that they do not even notice that you are going out of your way).

- Answering the phone or opening the door at home is a way of serving others.

- When you go on a backpacking trip there are always tasks that no one likes to do (like going to a creek to get water on a cold night, or starting up the fire). Be quick to offer yourself for such tasks.

- Take an interest in other people's things. It is always easier to plug in your headphones and listen to music than it is to talk with others and ask them about the things they like. Taking an interest in others requires a person to think less about "me, me, me" (my songs, my things), and to think more of others. Having a true and earnest concern for other people's things is a sign of maturity.

- If you are married, taking an interest in what your spouse and your children like, and having their concerns in mind during the day, is a sign of maturity.

In this area it is quite easy to fool oneself into thinking that to love consists not so much in doing things for others, but rather in understanding. One of the things that we learned in Chapter 1 is that any aspect of our inner life has to be expressed through our actions. We may understand others, but understanding is not true love. Understanding is at the foundation of love and is necessary for love to develop, but if it remains at that inner level, it is not true love.

For example, you may realize that your wife likes to read interior design magazines. You care nothing about interior design and, in fact, you find it hard to understand how anyone can waste time reading such literature. So you say to yourself, "Because I love my wife, even if I cannot understand how a human being can waste time reading those magazines, I will make an effort to be understanding, and I will not tell her that she is wasting her time."

This is fine, yet it is not true love. True love would require that you get interested in interior design magazines and, maybe, that one day you give her a little surprise by bringing home a magazine that she has never heard of (and that you discovered through your research, which took you a little bit of extra time).

Note that this does not require you to change your tastes. You may still not be interested in interior design, but, because your wife is, you make an effort to find what she likes. This is true love.

The same applies to the other types of love. If you have children, you will probably say that you love them. Your daughter Monica likes boats and you read in the newspaper that next weekend there is a boat show in town. You then think, "I am sure that Monica would like to go to the boat show. I don't know how anyone could waste a whole day looking at boats, but I will try to be understanding and I will not say anything if she wants to go." This is fine, yet it is not true love. True love would require you to find out the details of the boat show, offer to give her a ride, and spend time looking at the boats with her.

Beware of your "true love" if you are the kind of person who thinks that to love is above all to understand. Those who claim to understand others, but do not do much for them, should look at how much time and effort they spend thinking about and pursuing their own personal goals. You may find it absurd to spend a whole morning looking at boats, but perhaps you have no problem spending a whole morning playing golf. . .

Love is not about what you like or dislike, it is about showing through deeds that you are interested in others. True love is manifest in the daily sacrifice and renunciation for the other person, not in feelings and emotions.

The following is a great example of what it means to seek the good of the other. Dr. Laura Schlessinger is a psychologist who worked in private practice as a marriage counselor. She also started a radio program in which she answered questions from callers regarding their relationships. Julie, a listener of the program, related what "doing for" a husband actually does for the wife.

> Even if I am having a long day, too, I can pick up deli sandwiches, a container of soup, and some parsley. Planning my evening surprise for my husband, strangely, takes away my stress at work as well, because I'm thinking about someone else. At home I cut the sandwiches into triangles, stick fancy toothpicks through them, pour soup into bowls and add some garnish, set the table, and then greet him at the door with a big kiss and hug. How much time did this take? Five extra minutes. How much did we both receive? I had the opportunity to say in a small way, "We are a team and I support you," and he felt good that I had taken the extra time to make a simple thing beautiful just for him.[2]

Note that Julie did not have to wait for any sign of gratitude from him. She felt good simply as a result of her giving.

6.2   Thinking of Others

A person whose father died of a stroke will normally be concerned about cholesterol in everything he eats. He will have a "prejudice" with respect to cholesterol that you may not have. In an analogous way, true love gives the person a sort of "psychological prejudice" with regard to thinking of others. This psychological prejudice is a habit that we ought to acquire, for we are not born with it.

The ability to realize the needs of those around us is very important for the gift of self. If you miss the needs of your wife and your children, you are bound to a bitter marriage. If you miss the needs of your friends, you will only have acquaintances, not true friends. The habit of thinking of others can only be developed through daily practice.

- Whenever someone with this "prejudice" meets another person, he takes an interest in his family, his job, and his favorite team—he talks in terms of the others' interests. This does not mean that he does not talk about himself. He talks about his own matters with moderation, making sure that those who listen have a good time.

- He is happy to see that his friends are successful in whatever they do, and he encourages them. His happiness comes from seeing that others are happy.

- If he knows that there is something he can do for a friend, he takes the initiative and offers his help (instead of waiting until his help is requested).

- If he goes out with friends, instead of being concerned about himself having fun, he does everything in his power to ensure that his friends have fun.

- He lets others choose first. If there is chicken for dinner, he lets others choose the best parts. If he is eating pizza and there are several types, he lets others choose first.

- He takes interest in what his brothers and sisters are doing: sports, extra-curricular activities, friends... If his sister participates in a play, he goes to see her (not because his mother forces him to go, but because he really cares about his sister).

- If he is married, he takes interest in what his spouse is doing: hobbies, friends, family, and work. (The same applies to a woman who is married).

These are just a few examples. The reader will be able to find others that suit him better. One of the fruits of this "prejudice" with respect to thinking of others is cheerfulness, a virtue that is most important in order to enjoy true happiness.

Notes

[1] See J. Stenson, *Compass* (New York: Scepter, 2003), p. 20.

[2] L. Schlessinger, *The Proper Care and Feeding of Husbands* (New York: Harper Collins, 2004), pp. 18-19.

CHAPTER 7

Love and the Meaning of Shame

7.1 Shame

When Adam saw her for the first time, Eve was not dressed up, ready to go to a concert. They were both naked, yet they felt no shame. Seeing Eve naked, Adam did not lose sight of the fact that she was an "I", and vice versa. Adam and Eve were aware of their dignity, and they did not see each other as an object to be used. This is difficult to understand because we have never experienced that state of original innocence.

After Adam and Eve ate from the tree which God had asked them not to touch, they realized that they were naked, "so they sewed fig leaves together and made loincloths for themselves."[1] They did not cover their bodies because the weather had changed... Before the sin, Adam and Eve had a complete trust that the gift of self would be mutual, something like, "I trust that your nakedness is a sign that you want to live exclusively and permanently for me." There was no fear of being used; there was no fear of being looked at or desired lustfully.

After original sin they experienced the birth of lust, which must have been a shock for them. They experienced for the first time that the attraction of the bodies could stimulate something different than the union of the persons. The woman feared that the man would use her as a means to his own ends (as an object), and the man felt likewise with respect to the woman. So they covered their bodies.

Before original sin, nakedness did not express a lack; seeing the body, they could see the person. After original sin, nakedness began to express a lack; seeing the body, they lacked the vision of the person.

Shame has therefore a double dimension. On the one hand, it protects the person from lust by hiding the body. On the other hand, it enhances the person. By covering the sexual parts of the body, the person is saying something like, "I cover my body because I would like you to be aware that I am a person. I do not want you to come to my body, but to me." Shame exists in us to emphasize the nuptial meaning of the body.

7.2   Modesty

The tendency that shame generates in us to protect the core of our person is called modesty. Modesty is an intuition of the dignity proper to the person, an intuition of the capacity that each one has to make a complete gift of self.

Modesty refuses to unveil what should remain hidden. What belongs to our intimacy varies depending on the country or the geographical area, but in all cultures men and women protect their intimacy. Can you think of a place where people like to discuss family problems in public? In all cultures men and women refuse to unveil some parts of their inner life, and they cover the intimate parts of their body. (Shame does not only apply to the sexual sphere. A person who unnecessarily shares personal details of his inner life is also shameless).

Animals do not need to cover their bodies because, lacking an inner life, their bodies are not expression of an "I". A person's body, however, has the capacity to express his inner life.

Think of a woman who shows too much, or who wears revealing swimsuits, or who wears tight outfits that allow everyone to figure out "what should remain hidden." Her way of dressing cannot be part of the gift of self because such a gift requires exclusivity, while her dress is making her body the property of anyone who looks at her.

The habit of dressing immodestly damages the capacity of the woman to make a complete gift of herself. Because the essence of the person is realized in the gift of self, we say that the woman has "less personality." And the same applies to the man who dresses immodestly.

When talking about modesty, one may have the impression that there is certain asymmetry, for one one usually hears more about women's way of dressing than about men's. This is due to the fact that the sexual appetite expresses itself differently in men than in women. While women are more attracted by words and the sense of touch, men are more attracted by the sense of sight. Because a woman does not usually feel the urge to look lustfully at a man wearing trunks, she may find it hard to understand how a man can look lustfully at her wearing a bikini. She has to understand that in men, unlike in women, the sexual appetite gets turned on very fast by what they see.

For example, if a woman allows her underwear to be seen, or if she wears low cut dresses or tight outfits that reveal shapes and sizes, men will "look" at her. However, if a man lets his underwear be seen, women do not usually care much (they probably wonder how uncomfortable it must be to walk with the pants half way down).

Generally speaking, women have a greater need to please others, while men have a greater need to impress with physical strength and professional achievement. These differences are not absolutes, of course, but women should be aware of them because their tendency to please others may lead them to dress immodestly. They obviously perceive that men look at them and they feel good, but they have to be aware that these glances are frequently lustful.

> Men and women are quite different. A woman does not experience an automatic impulsive reaction of the flesh when she sees a man's body. A man does experience such a reaction when he sees a woman's body. Not being aware of this, many women interpret the glances of some men incorrectly. They think that the way they are looked at is due to admiration, that they are looked at as women and as persons; they do not know that, in many occasions, those glances are only directed to their body, considered as an object of sexual desire. There are many women who do not know that the male spontaneously tends to merely pay attention to the flesh, to what the woman has of an object. And that is why they make the mistake of calling men's attention by playing with what is purely sexual. Women would be greatly surprised if they knew what goes through the mind of the men who look at them, and the scorn that oftentimes they provoke in them.[2]

The parts of the body that better manifest the "I" are the head and the hands. The latter are so expressive that many people "talk with their hands." The closer an animal is to the human being, the more developed its hands are (compare a monkey with an elephant). And note how in all cultures, from the most ancient ones to our present day, people use jewelry to adorn their head (face and neck) and their hands.

Modesty should lead a woman to adorn the parts of her body that better manifest her personality and her virtues, and to cover the parts that would stir a male's appetites. When a woman reveals too much she is saying with her actions that she wants to attract men mainly because of her body, and not so much because of who she is.[3]

A woman is not completely responsible for how men look at her (she could be wrapped in a fur coat, and some obsessed maniac could still look at her lustfully). At the same time, the way a woman dresses reveals so much about her.

A woman's modesty ensures that the man is interested in her, and not only in her body. For a young man, one of the first things to look for in a young woman is that she dresses modestly, including when she goes to the pool or to the beach. Think of those women who dress light or too tight, whom everybody follows with their eyes, letting their thoughts go wild. Would you like a woman like that to be the mother of your children?

> Men can tell how much a woman respects herself by how she dresses (and by how she dances). If her sexual value is the first impression she gives to a man, she's inviting the type of guys who want to use her body... Modesty is a bold statement of your worth because it invites men to consider something deeper about you. It tells a guy that he can take you seriously as a woman, because you don't need to make boys gawk at you in order to feel secure. I'll grant that guys will stare at a girl who wears a short skirt that could be mistaken for a wide belt. But none of them respect her.[4]

7.3 Dating

In Section 4.2 we saw that one may be interested in a friend because he has free tickets to the football games. This need-love may provide the raw material for friendship, but true friendship will only develop if it is raised to the level of gift-love. An analogous thing happens with the love between a man and a woman.

You may be interested in a young woman because her dad is a billionaire, and you expect to have a big house in the future. This is not true love because you are not interested in her, but in your future. It may be that you are interested in a young woman because she is the prettiest on campus, and if you get to date her it will be a social success. This is not true love either, for you are just interested in showing your "trophy." You are thinking about yourself, not about her good.

For true love to develop there has to be physical and emotional attraction (*eros*). Part of this attraction may be that she is very popular on campus, or that "there is something in the way she smiles," or that "I feel something special when she is around." All these things are like the raw material for true love, which will only develop if these need-loves are raised to the level of gift-love.

One question that was asked to married people in a poll done in the United States was this: "Would you marry your spouse (again)?" 75 percent answered no! Seeing how people date (or, rather, hook up) today, the results of the poll are not surprising. When dating is just for fun, the sexual part blinds the eyes to the most important side of the other person (her virtues and the capacity to give herself completely). One of the key ideas of this section is that bad dating creates blind spots.

If you are going to give up your freedom to another person, you want to make sure that your future spouse has enough virtues to give himself or herself completely to you. The purpose of dating is to be a preparation for the exclusive and permanent gift of self that will take place in marriage.

Going steady should always be directed toward the complete gift of oneself. This does not mean that you will marry the first person you date. It means that you should only go steady with someone if you think that she could eventually be the mother of your children, or that he could be the father of your children. It may happen that it does not work out because you realize that she does not have enough virtues, or that some traits of her personality make it hard for you to adjust to her, or because she discovers that you have some defects that she does not like. That is what dating is for.[5]

Going steady should be directed toward commitment. If you go steady with someone just because it is fun, or because it is socially "cool," you would be using the other person as an object, and that relationship would not be true love.

The tendency to use the other person as an object for selfish gratification is stronger when one is physically close to that person. Close and frequent companionship between a man and a woman will always create many opportunities to use the other person. This frequent companionship is justified so long as it is oriented toward the gift of one's self; that is, as long as it is part of one's search for a spouse.

If one begins going steady without being in a position to marry, the frequent outcome is that one loses the idea of permanence and lifelong commitment associated with marriage. If you go steady with a person, and then you change to another one, and then to another, and then... it is like changing cars. When you get to marriage, you will unconsciously think that it is just another relationship.

When you fall in love, most of the things that you initially know about the other person are things that make you feel good. It is more about you than about her. A big hit of the Backstreet Boys in 1997 was "As long as you love me." This is what the chorus said:

> I don't care who you are
> Where you're from
> What you did
> As long as you love me.

Can you love a person without knowing who she really is? Unfortunately, this attitude is widespread today. Many movies, sitcoms, and songs convey that the stronger your feelings are, the stronger your love is. And that if you experience a strong feeling of love, the rest does not matter.

True love requires thinking about her good, and not so much about your feelings. One of the purposes of dating is precisely to find out about her family, her interests, the things that she likes, and so on. For instance, if she is interested in art, you can go with her to visit museums or exhibits, even if you do not like it that much. If he is interested in the outdoors, you may go out with him on a hike, even if you do not like it that much. Of course, if you also like museums and the outdoors, all the better.

You can discover a young woman's quality (a young man's quality is analogous) by the friends she has; by the heroes she admires; by the way she works; by looking at whether she is friendly to everyone, or only to people she can use; by how she treats people who wait on her or clean up after her (like janitors, waiters, bus drivers, people behind a counter); by what she talks about most often; or by how she treats her parents and siblings.[6]

One of the greatest mistakes that a man can make is to marry the wrong woman (and vice versa). If you like a young woman, ask yourself this question, "Is this the woman whom I would like to be the mother of my children?" If you are a young woman, ask yourself, "Is this the man whom I would like to be the father of my children?"

7.4   How Far is Too Far

"How far is too far" is not the right way to think about this issue. In Yosemite National Park many tourists go to the top of Half Dome and get close to the edge in order to see the fascinating view of the 2000-foot drop off... and some of them fall (to their death, of course). Nevertheless, the framework that has been developed in the previous chapters allows us to give an answer to that question.

As we have seen, the attraction of the bodies exits in us to stimulate the union of the persons. When sexual pleasure is used for purposes or in contexts other than the union of the persons, it does not respect the dignity of those involved because it becomes a lie. In order to experience pleasure, one needs to get sexually aroused. We may therefore consider an arousal as the first words in the language of the body when it wants to express union.

Before moving on, one clarification is needed. Experiencing an arousal does not represent by itself the first words of any language; it is just a biological process, oftentimes instinctive (in the case of men, for example, it is frequent to wake up being aroused). It is the consent of the will to seek sexual pleasure that makes it an action of the person. An arousal becomes the first words in the language of the body when there is consent to experience pleasure.

If one gets aroused and reacts quickly and quits, then there is no consent of the will. If there is consent (if one continues touching oneself), then the action constitutes a lie. It would be like the first words of a language that is meant to express union, while one knows that such union cannot exist. This lying to oneself is particularly selfish, for there is absolutely no element of giving.

The same applies when boyfriend and girlfriend exchange signs of affection, like holding hands, a simple kiss, an embrace, or a hug. If they are holding hands and one gets aroused, he should let go (the same applies if they are hugging or kissing). Otherwise, those signs of affection would not be an expression of true love, but rather a way of using the other person as an instrument for sexual gratification.

It was mentioned above that when we do not follow the "rules of use" that were created for our own good we damage ourselves. How does this happen? Sex before marriage, for example, does not damage the body (leaving aside sexually transmitted diseases, the biological action is healthy). What is damaged is our inner life. When sexual intercourse is not the external expression of the complete gift of self, the deep lie that is involved generates a strong inclination to use the other one as an object (and this harms the capacity of the person to give himself completely). Those who have sex before marriage have "less personality," in the sense that the fundamental characteristic of personal existence—the capacity to make a complete gift of self—is lessened in them.

The same applies to those who make out passionately, doing everything but not going "all the way." It also applies to the person who looks at pornography or who looks lustfully at others. These behaviors damage (some in a greater degree than others) the capacity of the person for true love, for giving himself completely.

Your goal should not just be to save sex for marriage, but to save yourself completely for your spouse. How would you feel if your future wife has already been passionately embracing other men? Or if she has already had sex with other men? If you are a young woman, how would you feel if your future husband has already been passionately embracing other women, or having sex with them? When you date, think of your future spouse, and how you are saving yourself for him or her.

> If you're going to get married one day, perhaps someone right now is dating the person you'll eventually marry. How far is too far for them? Practice the purity you would hope your future spouse would have, and treat your dates with the respect that you hope your future spouse would be given.[7]

Notes

[1] Genesis 3:7. References come from the St. Joseph Edition of the New American Bible.

[2] M. Gotzon, *Saber amar con el cuerpo* (Madrid: Palabra, 2005), pp. 72-73. The quotes from this work are my own translation.

[3] "If your heart is saying, 'Is this too short?' or 'Is this too tight?' listen to that intuition because it answered your question. Stand in front of a mirror and ask, 'What am I drawing attention to with this outfit? Is this outfit saying that the best thing about me is my body, or does it announce that I'm worth waiting to see?'" See J. Evert, *Pure Love* (San Diego: Catholic Answers, 2003), pp. 25-26.

[4] J. Evert, *Pure Love* (San Diego: Catholic Answers, 2003), p. 25.

[5] Good references about dating and marriage are J.R. Waiss, *Couples in Love* (New York: Crossroad, 2003); M.B. Bonacci, *Real Love* (San Francisco: Ignatius, 1996); and C. West, *Good News about Sex and Marriage* (Cincinnati: Servant, 2004). An excellent work, although not yet translated into English, is M. Gotzon, *Saber amar con el cuerpo* (Madrid: Palabra, 2005).

[6] See J. Stenson, *Compass* (New York: Scepter, 2003), p. 153. "If you are a young woman dating a guy who is disrespectful towards his mother and sisters, but is a perfect gentleman around you, guess what you have to look forward to if you settle down with him." See J. Evert, *If You Really Loved Me* (Ann Arbor: Servant, 2003), p. 47.

[7] J. Evert, *Pure Love* (San Diego: Catholic Answers, 2003), pp. 12-13.

CHAPTER 8

Love and Loyalty

8.1   The Law of the Gift

Vince is watching the World Series and Kim asks him for help to put the kids to bed. Following his wife's request, Vince gives up the baseball game and gives her a hand. This is an example of what it means to raise one's behavior to the level of the gift. When they got married, Vince said to Kim something like, "I surrender my freedom to you because I want to live exclusively and permanently for you." True love between a man and a woman develops when every aspect of their relationship is raised to the level of the gift.

Before getting married a man can go wherever he wants, he can paint the walls of his apartment bright orange, he can eat whenever he wants, and he can spend his money however he wants. But one day he marries, and he gives up many of these "freedoms." From that moment on, his time, his plans, his dreams, his projects, his money, his professional goals, and everything that he has belongs no more to himself. He freely decides to subordinate everything to the good of his wife. This is the Law of the Gift.[1]

He does not abandon his projects, his hobbies, his dreams, his plans, or his professional goals. He puts them in a new perspective; he puts them at the service of the communion of persons. The reference point for everything that he does shifts from himself to his wife, and the reference point for everything that she does shifts from herself to her husband. This is the union that takes place in marriage.

> True love develops when every aspect of one's life is raised to the level of the complete gift of one's self.

One of the keys of true love is to place the needs of the beloved above one's own, in full confidence that one's own needs will be met by the beloved.

To place the needs of your spouse above your own means to give your self away, and this makes you vulnerable. If you avoid being excessively concerned about yourself in order to be concerned about your spouse, but then he or she does not care about meeting your needs, you will feel abandoned and enslaved. If this happens, you may develop over time a natural fear of "letting go," and this will end up cooling the relationship and becoming a source of unhappiness.

To place the needs of others above one's own is not easy, especially in a society that has elevated feelings over commitment and sacrifice. Placing the needs of others above one's own in a consistent way requires fortitude, temperance, humility, and generosity. It also requires loyalty.

8.2 Loyalty

In the second century B.C. there was an attempt to suppress Judaism from Palestine and the Jews were persecuted.

Many of them were forced by the king either to reject their Jewish faith or to die.

> Eleazar, one of the foremost scribes, a man of advanced age and noble appearance, was being forced to open his mouth to eat pork. But preferring a glorious death to a life of defilement, he spat out the meat, and went forward of his own accord to the instrument of torture... Those in charge of that unlawful ritual meal took the man aside privately, because of their long acquaintance with him, and urged him to bring meat of his own providing, such as he could legitimately eat, and to pretend to be eating some of the meat of the sacrifice prescribed by the king; in this way he would escape the death penalty, and be treated kindly because of their old friendship with him.

> But he made up his mind in a noble manner, worthy of his years, the dignity of his advanced age, the merited distinction of his gray hair, and of the admirable life he had lived from childhood; and so he declared that above all he would be loyal to the holy laws given by God.

> He told them to send him at once to the abode of the dead, explaining: "At our age it would be unbecoming to make such a pretense; many young men would think the ninety-year-old Eleazar had gone over to an alien religion. Should I thus dissimulate for the sake of a brief moment of life, they would be led astray by me, while I would bring shame and dishonor on my old age. Even if, for the time being, I avoid the punishment of men, I shall never, whether alive or dead, escape the hands of the Almighty. Therefore, by manfully giving up my life now, I will

prove myself worthy of my old age, and I will leave to the young a noble example of how to die willingly and generously for the revered and holy laws."

He spoke thus, and went immediately to the instrument of torture. Those who shortly before had been kindly disposed now became hostile toward him because what he had said seemed to them utter madness. When he was about to die under the blows, he groaned and said: "The Lord in his holy knowledge knows full well that although I could have escaped death, I am not only enduring terrible pain in my body from this scourging, but also suffering it with joy in my soul because of my devotion to him." This is how he died, leaving in his death a model of courage and an unforgettable example of virtue not only for the young but for the whole nation.[2]

This is an outstanding example of loyalty, the virtue by which we remain faithful to our commitments and promises, even in the face of adversity or difficulty.

We acquire loyalty by practicing in small things. If you agree to go out with a friend and someone else calls with a more interesting plan, honor your commitment and go out with your friend. If you agreed to go shopping with your wife on Saturday morning and your friends call saying that they are playing golf... do not try to find complicated excuses; be loyal to your wife. Another manifestation of loyalty is never to talk badly about our friends; and never to let others talk badly about them if they are not present. It is only by practicing in small things that one can build up the loyalty that will be needed in more important occasions.

The gift of self is a promise: "From today on I belong to you, and I want to live this way every day of my life." Getting married is only the beginning of a path of self-giving. After the wedding, husband and wife have to give themselves to each other every single day. The external ceremony of getting married does not imply by itself that the spouses are giving themselves completely. The gift of self starts with the wedding ceremony, but the spouses have to make it happen every day of their lives.

When we turn a computer on we expect it to be ready in a few seconds—if it takes longer we usually get impatient. When we buy a new car we expect it to be maintenance free for a long time. Likewise, many people expect marriage to be free of difficulties, and when they meet the first ones they think that their decision was wrong; that he should not have married that woman; that she should not have married that man; that they should have waited longer to marry; and so on.

When we commit to someone we ought to be loyal and endure the difficulties, which can have a beneficial influence on our lives. It is precisely by overcoming them that we mature and we get to reap the fruits of true love. A life without difficulties has little heroism. Without difficulties we do not have many opportunities to show true love.

8.3 Marriage and Loyalty

If I give my car to a friend and he gets tired of it, he could return the car. In an analogous way, one could conclude that, when a man and a woman give themselves to each other, one of the spouses could return the gift if things were to go wrong. Divorce would have the effect of returning the "I" to the other spouse: "You gave me your self, but I have grown tired of it and I give it back; from now on you can do with it whatever you want."

This conclusion is not correct because the "I" is not something that one has. The "I" is what defines the person who has. The other person cannot return my "I" because she does not have it as she has a belt. What the other person has is my commitment to place her needs above my own until death do us part.

The gift that takes place in marriage is not of the type "I give you this," but rather "I commit to this." Marriage does not consist in giving things, but in giving the "I". Marriage does not stem from the wedding ceremony nor from the legal paperwork, but from the will of the spouses to commit in an exclusive and permanent way.[3]

Marriage takes place when the decision is irrevocable; if there is no such commitment, there is no marriage bond. The legal union is just a record that is kept in a room or in a computer. Divorce is the dissolution of such record and, therefore, it is something that happens at a legal level.

The marriage bond, however, exists at the level of the person. Vince could get divorced and find another woman, but, as long as Kim is alive, "being Vince" will always include "being for Kim." Trying to give himself to another woman may include some element of giving, but it will not contribute to his development as a person (at least as much as giving himself to Kim would have). The man who divorces his wife and marries another woman lessens the core of his person in a profound way because the fundamental characteristic of personal existence—the capacity to make a gift of self—is deeply damaged. (The same applies to the woman who divorces her husband).

The degree of giving that is required by the gift of self may produce dizziness or vertigo. However (and paradoxically), this self-giving constitutes the foundation of true love. After the original decision, one ought to develop the virtue of loyalty so that the gift of self becomes a reality.

8.4 Giving Oneself to God

In Chapter 4 we saw that to give oneself completely means to limit one's freedom in order to unite one's will with the beloved's will. It follows that, by uniting his will to God's will, anyone can give himself completely to God. For most people, God's will includes finding a spouse and being married to him or her during their lives. Being married is not an obstacle to giving oneself to God.

In order to understand this better, consider for a moment the motives of our actions. If you have a job, you may work in order to make money and buy an expensive car, or to help the company you work for. Both motives are not mutually exclusive. You may have a personal interest in the company, and in this case your motivation will also include (besides making money) the good of the company.

You may also work for other motives, like the professional recognition that you achieve, the challenge of solving problems, the trips to other countries, or the new people that you meet.

If you are married, the main motive of your work will be to support your family. The *immediate* motive may be to achieve professional recognition, but the *ultimate* motive is your family. Our actions usually have multiple motives, and there is a hierarchy among them.

Vince has agreed with his wife to take their daughter to piano lessons on Wednesday evenings. One Wednesday he comes home with a strong headache, and his wife offers to take the girl to the piano class. A first motive of her actions is to make sure that her daughter does not miss the lesson; another motive is to make sure that her husband can rest. Both are perfectly compatible. The immediate motive of Kim's actions is her daughter, while the ultimate motive is her husband.

In an analogous way, when a person gives himself completely to his spouse, the immediate motive of the gift of self
is his spouse, but the ultimate motive may well be God. A
married person can give himself completely to God if (among
another things) the ultimate reason of the gift of self to his
spouse is God. When a married person gives himself to God,
we say that he does it *through* his spouse.

With his own life, Christ introduced a new way of living
the nuptial meaning of the body, namely, to anticipate on
earth the gift of self that will take place in heaven between
God and man. This is called "apostolic celibacy."

Before Christ, there had been many people who did not
marry, but this had been due to different reasons. For the
Jewish people marriage had a sacred meaning because of
God's promise to Abraham (Genesis 17:4-7). The Jews knew
that the Messiah would be the "son of David," so marriage
was a privileged state, a state that worked toward the ful-
fillment of the kingdom of God. To renounce marriage for
the kingdom of heaven made no sense to them.[4]

In fact, Christ's life was probably difficult to understand
for the citizens of Nazareth, especially for those with daughters of Jesus' age. His own friends were probably surprised
that he did not date, and that his twenties were going by
and he was not doing anything to marry. They could not realize that Jesus was already living on earth the communion
with God in which we are called to live for all eternity.

Before moving on, it is convenient to make explicit the
meaning of the following terms:

- *Celibacy* means not being married. Celibacy in itself
  does not bear the imprint of likeness to Christ. This
  only happens when celibacy is chosen voluntarily and
  for the kingdom of God, which is what we call "apostolic celibacy."[5]

- *Continence* means abstention from sexual intercourse. A married couple may live continence for a period, which means that they abstain from having sexual relations during that period. A person who is celibate should be continent until he marries. Someone who has sex with his girlfriend is celibate, but not continent. A person who has chosen apostolic celibacy should live perpetual continence.

- *Virginity* refers to a biological fact. A person who has not had sexual intercourse is a virgin. A person who is not a virgin but later decides to become a priest (like St. Augustine) will live continence from then on.

Apostolic celibacy is not equal to "not marrying," or "not having sex," or "not having children." It means to give oneself exclusively to God in this life. By renouncing marriage, one can dedicate all his energies with an undivided heart to bringing to others the kingdom of heaven.

The most attractive aspect of apostolic celibacy, however, is the great intimacy with the Trinity that this vocation allows on earth. Apostolic celibacy is living the nuptial meaning of the body as Jesus lived it, allowing the person to live in a very intimate communion with the Trinity.

> The achievement of this kingdom must be found along the line of the authentic development of the image and likeness of God in its Trinitarian meaning, that is, precisely of communion. By choosing continence for the kingdom of heaven, man has the knowledge of being able in that way to fulfill himself differently and, in a certain way, more than through matrimony, becoming a "true gift to others."[6]

Apostolic celibacy is a high calling not because those who choose it abstain from sexual intercourse. What makes apos-

tolic celibacy such a high calling is the fact of renouncing
something which is good (marriage and family) in order to
contribute in a greater way to the kingdom of heaven.

This is why the Church has always held that apostolic
celibacy is a higher calling than marriage. "Not by reason of
inferiority, nor with prejudice against the conjugal union of
the body," but because it allows a person to imitate Christ
more closely.[7] Such is the meaning of the following words
that were cited on the previous page: "By choosing continence for the kingdom of heaven, man has the knowledge of
being able in that way to fulfill himself differently and, in
a certain way, more than through matrimony, becoming a
true gift to others."

While apostolic celibacy is objectively a higher calling,
what is better for the individual person is what God calls
him to. The quality of our love does not depend on whether
we have sexual intercourse or not; it depends on how much
we give ourselves. The person who gives himself fully and
generously to his spouse, accepting the children that may
come as a consequence of the completeness of the gift, will
reach a high love. The priest, the lay celibate, or the religious who becomes lukewarm and leads a life of comfort and
selfishness will not reach such a high love.

As in marriage, one of the keys of apostolic celibacy is to
place the beloved's needs above one's own, in full confidence
that one's needs will be met by him. This requires the person
not to be excessively concerned about himself, trusting that
God will take care of his needs.

When one gives himself exclusively to God, he subordi-
nates his time, his plans, his dreams, his projects, his hobbies, and his professional goals to the good of the kingdom
of heaven. He does not necessarily abandon his dreams, his
projects, his hobbies, or his goals. He puts them in a new
perspective. In some cases, one has to abandon his profes-

sion or some of his professional goals. But even in those cases that do not imply a professional change, one ought to put everything at the service of the kingdom of God. Apostolic celibacy is not "professional celibacy."

Betrothed love requires reciprocity, which points to the deep union with God that apostolic celibacy allows.[8] This intimacy makes attractive the renunciation of marriage and forming a family in order to contribute in a more intense way toward the realization of the kingdom of God.

Marriage is the normal path for man to make a complete gift of himself; apostolic celibacy is an exception to this general rule. Apostolic celibacy is a counsel, not a command.[9] A few months before his death, this is what John Paul II said to a group of young people from Switzerland:

> If this is your vocation, giving your life to Christ with an undivided heart, you will be able to be an undaunted and unflagging apostle... Yes, you too can be one of these! I am well aware that you may feel hesitant when faced with such a proposal; but I say to you: do not be afraid! God does not let himself be outdone in generosity! After almost 60 years of being a priest, I am happy to bear my witness to all of you here: it is beautiful to be able to spend oneself without reserve for the cause of the Kingdom of God![10]

8.5 Loyalty and the Gift of Self

One day the garage door does not open, and Vince thinks that the best solution is to spend a few hours on Saturday trying to fix it. Kim knows that if he tries to fix the door, Vince will spend the whole day working on it. As she would like to go out for dinner and to watch a movie, she says, "Honey, maybe we could call a repair company and have someone come to fix the door, so that on Saturday we can go out for dinner and watch a movie." Vince thinks that his way is the best way to solve the problem (and, besides, it will be cheaper), so he insists on working on the door...

By the end of Saturday, they have not gone out and they end up having dinner at home. Most of the time, these issues have nothing to do with efficiency or with saving money; they have to do with the fact that "this is my idea, this is my way of doing things."

The day they married, Vince promised to give his wife everything he had, including his efficient ways of fixing garage doors. The most difficult part of the gift of self is to surrender the innermost aspects of the "I", namely, our intelligence and our will.

As it was mentioned in Section 4.3, the key is not so much the negative aspect of limiting one's freedom, but rather the positive one of uniting our will to the beloved's will. This turns out to be difficult because our intelligence and our will are at the core of who we are, and giving them away is like giving ourselves away.

In the first stages of marriage, the gift of self is usually surrounded by abundant feelings and intense emotions that are fueled by sensuality. During the first stages of married life (as well as during courtship) one has to be careful not to confuse feelings with true love.

> It is impossible to judge the value of a relationship between persons merely from the intensity of their emotions. The very exuberance of the emotions born of sensuality may conceal an absence of true love, or indeed outright egoism. Love is one thing, and erotic sensations are another. Love develops on the basis

of a fully committed and fully responsible attitude
of a person to a person, erotic experiences are born
spontaneously from sensual and emotional reactions.
A very rich and rapid growth of such sensations may
conceal a love which has failed to develop.[11]

When a couple wants to examine how their marriage is going,
each spouse should look at himself (not at the other one)
and evaluate sincerely how he is placing the other's needs
above his own. When feelings and emotions taper off one
may have the impression that love has evaporated because
of the absence of feelings, or their lower intensity. However,
the test of love is not abundance of feelings, but rather how
the spouses are giving themselves to each other.[12]

In the case of older couples who have been married for
decades, it may give the impression that there is not much
love, but this is a false appearance. Their love lies in the
synchronization of their wills, in the fact that over the years
each one has acquired a habit of being unselfishly concerned
about the other, and this habit has become second nature.

Besides the will, one must also surrender the intelligence.
This is one of the most difficult aspects of the gift of self. To
surrender one's intelligence does not mean that one should
not use it. It means that one should raise it to the level of
the gift.

Many scientists were convinced for centuries that the sun
revolved around the earth, but they were wrong. This example shows that to feel sure about something does not mean
that it is true. To feel sure that one's wife will never change
does not mean that she will not change; to feel sure that the
one who has problems is the other spouse does not mean
that things are that way; and so on.

If a man does not want to be any more with the woman
whom he married, his determined will may force his intelli-

gence to believe that "things are as I see them." Most likely
he is only seeing a portion of reality. The will to leave his
wife can "bend" his intelligence so that it only looks at the
portion of reality that he is interested in seeing. However,
the ultimate reference point is not our intelligence, but the
gift of self. Only those actions that are raised to the level of
the gift can become an expression of true love.

A man may decide to leave his wife because he clearly
sees that he should not continue with her. A priest or a lay
celibate may decide to leave his vocation because he clearly
sees that he should not continue with it. "I see things now
in a different way. I am convinced that a person cannot renounce his own vision of reality in order to do what others
tell him to do. I will never renounce thinking for myself and
looking at things as I see them." Acting and making decisions because "this is how I see it" may be intellectually
rewarding, but if the actions that follow from the "clear vision" are not raised to the level of the gift, they will have
the effect of reducing one's capacity to love.

Following one's intelligence is not necessarily a sign of
true love. At the bottom of most broken marriages and lacks
of perseverance of those who give themselves exclusively to
God, there is a determination of not giving some of the
deeper aspects of one's self.

Lack of loyalty does not happen suddenly. A person does
not happily live with his spouse, wake up one day, and decide
to leave her. Gift-love is a virtue, and it has to develop day
by day. Some people will have to work on temperance, some
on fortitude, others on humility, and others on generosity. If
these daily acts of giving do not take place, time will go by
and one day the person may discover that he does not love
with enough intensity to keep his promises. He has lost the
freedom of the gift, and no longer has the capacity to make
a complete gift of himself.

8.6 The Law of the Gift Is for Everybody

The universe is ruled by laws that reflect the way in which it was created. Some of them, called *physical* laws, apply to all material beings just because of the fact that they are material—the law of gravity, for example, equally applies to things, animals, and man. Other laws (like the law of growth or the law of aging) only apply to living beings, and they are referred to as *biological* laws. Others apply exclusively to human beings, such as the laws against murder or those that protect private property; these are referred to as the *moral* law, and they tell man how to behave according to the way he was created.

Recall the example of the microwave from Section 3.3. The instructions of use were not imposed on the microwave after it was built. They were built in it, and they reflect the way in which the manufacturer wired the electronic circuits and components. Without these circuits and components, the microwave would not work.

In the same way, the moral law was not imposed on us after we were born; it is built in us. It reflects something that was imprinted on our nature. As the microwave is rendered useless if the rules of use are not respected, the person is also rendered "useless" (incapable of happiness) if he does not follow the moral law.

If the lady knew that putting the dog in the microwave would be fatal to the dog, her action would be considered an offense against the dog. If she was not aware of the fatal effects, there would be no offense... but the effects on the dog would be equally devastating!

Something similar happens with our actions. One of the rules of use of the human being is fidelity in marriage. If the person who commits adultery knows this law, he would sin because he would be going against God's will. If he is not aware of the command, his action would not be sinful, but he would still suffer tremendous damage as a person.[13]

Fidelity in marriage is best for man because adultery is a deep lie. You may not like the law, but that does not mean that it will not apply to you. (The dog will explode in the microwave independent of whether you know who made the microwave, or whether you know its rules of use). If you commit adultery, the core of your person will be damaged independent of whether you know God or the moral law.[14]

If a Christian, a Buddhist, a Jew, a Muslim, or an atheist jump off a high cliff... they will equally fall. In fact, they will all fall with the same acceleration. Only their speed will be different, but this has to do with their size—not with their religious convictions. In the same way, the Law of the Gift is not a "religious" law, for the notions of exclusivity and permanence apply to all human beings, independent of their culture, religion, or race.

Notes

[1] The name comes from the title of the article by E. Sri, "The Law of the Gift" in *Lay Witness*, Sept-Oct (2005), pp. 24–25, 51.

[2] 2 Maccabees 6:18-31.

[3] In the case of the Catholic sacrament, the presence of the priest plus two witnesses is required; but "if after a month there is no one to act as qualified witness [priest], it is enough the presence of two other witnesses. And if the couple is romantically lost in an island, it will be enough their mutual commitment. This couple would be really married—also 'by the Church', with the sacrament if they are Catholic—, even if no one else knows about it. Because the essential element is the 'yes' that is freely given, not the ceremonies or the paperwork." See M. Gotzon, *Saber amar con el cuerpo* (Madrid: Palabra, 2005), p. 35.

[4] In the Old Testament there are no examples of people who lived apostolic celibacy. The prophet Jeremiah did not choose celibacy for the kingdom of God; he was asked by God not to marry because of the danger of raising children in his circumstances. "The sons and daughters who will be born in this place... of deadly disease they shall die... For I have withdrawn my friendship with this people, says the Lord... They shall die, the great and the lowly, in this land and shall go unburied and unlamented" (Jeremiah 16:3-6). See John Paul II, *The Theology of the Body* (Boston: Pauline, 1997), p. 265, as well as footnote 95 on p. 302 [Mar. 17, 1982].

[5] Some people may be called to give themselves completely through other paths, like the person who decides not to marry in order to care for his dying parents, or for a sibling with Down Syndrome. These cases are not apostolic celibacy, but they can also provide a way to make a complete gift of one's self.

[6] John Paul II, *The Theology of the Body* (Boston: Pauline, 1997), pp. 273-274 [Apr. 7, 1982].

[7] There has always been a strong tendency to associate the source of evil with matter. This way of thinking, which is called *Manichaeism*, considers the body and everything that is corporeal in man as a source of evil. As sex is part of the body, Manichaeism considers sex and *eros* as something bad or dirty, a sort of necessary evil in order to facilitate procreation. We have seen that there is no contraposition between erotic love and gift-love; both are good. Christ "proposes to his disciples the ideal of continence and the call to it, not by reason of inferiority, nor with prejudice against the conjugal union of the body, but only for the sake of the kingdom of heaven." See John Paul II, *The Theology of the Body* (Boston: Pauline, 1997), p. 276 [Apr. 14, 1982].

[8] When a man and woman get married, there is a union of persons. In an analogous manner (not physically, but in a spiritual manner) the person who lives apostolic celibacy becomes one with God in a very special way. "For the Lord delights in you... As a young man marries a virgin, your Builder shall marry

you; and as a bridegroom rejoices in his bride, so shall your God rejoice in you" (Isaiah 62:4-5).

[9] "He who marries does well, and he who refrains from marriage will do better" (1 Cor 7:38).

[10] John Paul II, *Meeting with Swiss Youth,* June 6, 2004.

[11] K. Wojtyla, *Love and Responsibility* (San Francisco: Ignatius, 1993), p. 145.

[12] Something analogous happens with apostolic celibacy. In the first stages of one's vocation, the gift of self is usually nurtured by abundant feelings and enthusiasm, and one has to be careful not to confuse feelings and enthusiasm with true love.

[13] The laws that rule the universe were designed for our good. When we decide not to follow them, we are saying with our actions that we care little about God's love for us. This "not caring" is sin. For an action to be sinful there must be *knowledge* that the action goes against God's law, and *consent* of the will. (If you are forced to pull a gun's trigger, the death that may follow is not willed by you). When we sin we damage ourselves, and this is why it is so painful for God, who desires our good more than any parent desires his children's good. The fact that God suffers is difficult to understand. It is a suffering that comes from love. It is analogous to a person who loves someone intensely, and sees that the beloved is suffering. When a mother learns that her child was involved in a serious accident, she does not suffer from physical pain, she suffers because her child is suffering.

[14] When Matt becomes a priest or Cristina gives her life exclusively to God, a new relationship qualifies who they are. Matt could abandon the priesthood, but once ordained, being Matt will always include being exclusively for God. Cristina could abandon her vocation, but, once the commitment is permanent, being Cristina will always include being exclusively for God. Looking for another path may include some element of giving, but it will not contribute to their development as persons (at least as much as being faithful to their vocation would have). One may ignore the Law of the Gift, but one cannot break it.

CHAPTER 9

Love and Forgiveness

What happens if you realize that so far your love has not been true love, or that you have not loved much? Something that follows from the previous chapters is that it is never too late to start loving. Although one may have acquired habits that make the gift of self a difficult task, these habits can be reversed. Oftentimes this is not easy, and it requires hard work, but it is always possible.

If someone owes you $1000 and he pays you back, it was his duty to give you back the money. If someone who does not owe you anything gives you $1000, you will surely be grateful because you have received something you were not entitled to. In the same way, if you owe someone $1000 and he forgives the debt, you will also be grateful, for you have received something you did not deserve. The gratitude we experience when we receive something undeserved inclines us to love the giver even more. A very powerful reason to love is to experience forgiveness.

Asking for forgiveness is a necessary step, but it may not be enough because with our past behavior we will have developed stable dispositions or inclinations that are incompatible with giving ourselves completely. We may have developed the habit, for instance, of placing our needs above others' needs, or of using others as a means to our own ends. Lack of true love may also come from an acquired habit of exclusively thinking about oneself; or from an addiction to alcohol or to anger; or from using the appetites in an incorrect way; or simply from pride.

True love is not like a switch—you flip it up and immediately the light turns on, you flip it down and immediately the light turns off. True love requires time because virtue is not a one-time deal. If you have developed bad habits in the past, you will have to work hard to overcome them and acquire the virtues that will allow you to give yourself completely—and this requires time.

Even if the gift of self has not been complete, in the course of your life you have made—for sure—acts of generosity, as well as acts of the other virtues, and you can build upon these to develop deeper habits.

In order to give ourselves completely we need fortitude, temperance, generosity, sincerity (to recognize our wrongdoings), and humility (to ask for forgiveness). Another virtue that we need is prudence. Prudence is sometimes understood as being shrewd or cunning, but this is an erroneous notion. Prudence is the ability to make right judgments. For example, prudence is used in choosing our friends, what career we follow, or what businesses we participate in; it is also used when choosing what places we go to, or what parties we attend; prudence is exercised as well when choosing a date or a spouse.

A manifestation of prudence is to ask for advice. It goes without saying that one should ask for the advice of those who are wise. If one goes through a difficult relationship, through a separation, or through a divorce, returning to the path of true love may be difficult. Without advice it is almost impossible. There are some situations in which a couple needs the professional advice of a psychologist or a marriage counselor. Seeking this advice is an act of prudence. Prudence is very important for true love.

If for whatever reason your love so far has not been true love, think carefully about what has been missing. What are you lacking to make a complete gift of yourself? To get back (or started) on the path of true love, you may need to begin by asking others for forgiveness. You should then make concrete resolutions to develop the basic virtues, use those virtues to give yourself in small things, and little by little develop a habit of self-giving. This process may be hard, but it is available to all who are humble enough to recognize their mistakes.

So far we have talked about asking for forgiveness. We finish this chapter with a word about forgiving others. A person who keeps a list of offenses ("Three days ago you said this, and a week ago you told me that, and a year ago you did not say hello when I got back home, and three years ago you would not listen to me") should realize that this is one more way of having. True love requires giving ourselves completely, and this includes any list of offenses we may keep. A great manifestation of true love is to forgive.

CHAPTER **10**

Love and Freedom

10.1 Freedom and Commitment

Soon after the attack on September 11, 2001, a man boarded
an airplane with a bomb built into his shoe. His name was
Richard Reid, and he was brought before the court in Jan-
uary 2003. After admitting his guilt, as well as his allegiance
to Osama bin Laden, he added, "I think I will not apologize
for my actions. I am at war with your country." He was sen-
tenced to life in prison. The judge, William Young, delivered
a statement in which he talked about terrorism and freedom.

> Here, in this society, the very wind carries freedom.
> It carries it everywhere from sea to shining sea. It
> is because we prize individual freedom so much that
> you are here in this beautiful courtroom. So that ev-
> eryone can see, truly see, that justice is administered
> fairly, individually, and discretely...It seems to me
> you hate the one thing that to us is most precious.
> You hate our freedom. Our individual freedom. Our

> individual freedom to live as we choose, to come and
> go as we choose, to believe or not believe as we in-
> dividually choose.[1]

When someone who has been in prison is released, we say
that he has been freed. When a lion is let out of the cage, we
say that the lion is free. One could therefore get the idea that
freedom is the capacity "to live as we choose, to come and go
as we choose, and to believe or not believe as we individually
choose." This, however, is a poor notion of freedom.

If you have a job, you cannot go wherever you want during the week because you are subject to a schedule. Would
you say that you are not free? The day they got married,
Vince and Kim committed themselves to one another. From
that day on, they cannot rightfully go out on dates with
whomever they want. Would you say that they are not free
because they are committed to each other?

To understand freedom as the possibility to do whatever
I want, to live as I choose, to say what I please, or to think
what I want, is to understand freedom in a negative way (as
"I don't want to have restrictions on my behavior," or "I
don't want to commit because it would limit my options").

You are considering whether to buy a Honda, a Toyota,
a Volkswagen, or a Chevy. You finally decide on the Honda,
which means that you are saying no to the other cars. Is
your freedom reduced because you chose the Honda?

You decide to major in Political Science. You are saying no to majoring in English Literature, in Economics, in
Psychology, in Math, in Physics... Is your freedom reduced
because you chose Political Science?

When a woman marries a man she is saying no to all
other men. Is her freedom reduced because of her choice?

The first thing we can deduce from these examples is
that when we exercise our freedom we exclude many alter-

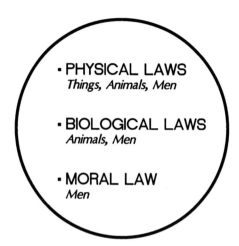

natives. Exercising one's freedom requires commitment, and this always entails ruling out other possibilities.

As we saw in Section 8.6, the universe is ruled by laws that reflect the way in which it was created, namely, the physical laws, the biological laws, and the moral law. There is a very important difference, however, between these types of laws. If we jump off a cliff, we do not have a choice regarding whether or not we fall, and as we grow up we do not have a choice regarding whether or not we age. We cannot escape the physical and biological laws; however, we are not forced to follow the moral law. Man has the capacity to choose what is right, what is truly human. That is freedom.

> Freedom is the capacity to choose what is right.

When we make poor use of our freedom we lessen the core of our person. It is like putting the dog in the microwave; we can do it, but it will render the microwave useless.

10.2   True Freedom

Animals have freedom of movement. Birds, for example, have the freedom to fly wherever they want. How does this compare to the freedom that we enjoy?

Animals receive a variety of impressions through the external senses and the memory, and their appetites react to these sense impressions by moving the animal to act in a specific way. When a sheep sees a wolf, the sheep judges it as harmful and flees from the wolf. This judgment (which may be called "natural judgment") is necessarily determined in a specific way because it has to do with particular things. The sheep can only apprehend this danger or that danger, this evil or that evil, but not the notions of danger and evil.

Human beings, however, have two powers that move them to action. On the one hand, the appetites, which react to the impressions that we sense or imagine; and on the other hand, the will, which is moved by the good.

The key point is that our intellect allows us to grasp universal notions. Not only do we grasp this good or that good, but also the notion of good itself. Universal notions (like the notion of good) can be applied to many different things or actions. Therefore, the judgment of the intellect regarding what is good for man is not necessarily determined toward one of those actions.

For instance, when an animal is hungry, the appetite moves it to look for food (its "natural judgment" determines that eating now is good). When a person is hungry the appetite also inclines him to eat, but the intellect may judge that eating now would ruin his figure, so "not eating" is presented to the will under the aspect of good. Animals have freedom of movement and action, but they do not have the freedom of judgment that we have.

While the animal is necessarily moved to eat, the person can choose. While the source of the animal's actions lies in external things (the food that stimulates its appetite), the source of the person's actions lies within himself (in his intelligence, that may judge it to be worth not eating in order to be in shape). Animals are not truly free because they are not themselves the source of their actual moving, which is rather determined by the impressions that they sense or that are retrieved from their memory. The person is free because he is the source of his actual moving. This is explained in more detail in the following paragraphs.

Once an object produces an impression on the senses, the appetite judges whether it is good or bad for the appetite (whether it is pleasurable or not). This judgment is called "natural judgment" because it is determined by nature. The actions that are pleasurable to our senses are determined by nature, and they are common to all individuals. If the action is pleasurable, the appetite will necessarily judge it as good and will arouse a strong desire for it; if the action is harmful, the appetite will necessarily judge it as bad and will shun it. If a fish is hungry and sees the bait, it can only bite it; if the sheep sees the wolf, the sheep can only flee.

This is why animals are not themselves the source of their actual moving. Animals are moved by what they sense because the appetites are necessarily moved by the impressions that they receive (together with "natural judgment").

As far as the appetites move their limbs, animals surpass inanimate objects and plants in that they have freedom of movement. But they do not have freedom of judgment. Because they have to follow the appetites, animals are not masters of their own actions, and thus are not truly free.

While the appetites are moved by what they receive from the senses (or from the memory), the will is moved by what it receives from the intellect. As the intellect can grasp the notion of good itself present in all things, the judgment of our intellect is not necessarily determined to this good or that good (as "natural judgment" is), and it can therefore present a variety of courses of action to the will under some aspect of good. Because the will can be inclined to anything that is presented to it under the aspect of good, intellectual beings have freedom of choice.

The actions of free beings proceed from the judgment that something is good (the will makes the decision to pursue something once the intellect has judged it to be good). However, this judgment does not necessarily have to be right.

The key point is to realize that the universal notion of good can be found in everything. There is not one single thing that can be said to be pure evil (this is the first principle that we discussed in Section 3.3, that "all created things are good"). This principle comes from the fact that evil is not a thing, but rather the absence of good.

Because the notion of good can be found in everything and our intellect has the capacity to grasp it, it follows that the intellect can present to the will under the aspect of good something that is not right for the person.

For example, if a married man notices that a female coworker is interested in him, his intellect may judge adultery as something good (it will be enjoyable). In this case the intellect's judgment would be wrong. Being unfaithful to one's spouse is bad for the person because it is a lie. And when we lie, we damage ourselves.

If you take your dog for a walk and it rains, your intellect may judge that putting the dog in the microwave is something good (the dog would dry off, you think). In this case the intellect's judgment would also be wrong.

Note that in the first example the judgment is wrong because the action (adultery) goes against the moral law, while in the example of the dog the judgment is wrong because the action goes against physical and biological laws.

The "natural judgment" can only declare good what is right for the appetite (if you are hungry, the appetite cannot move you to fast). The will, however, has the *capacity* to choose what is right for the person, but is not necessarily moved to it. This is what freedom of choice means. Free beings have the capacity to choose what is right, and that capacity is true freedom.

If one denies the existence of right and wrong as something objective, then true freedom loses its meaning. If there is no right and wrong, what does it mean "to choose what is right"? Freedom in this case would just be the capacity to do whatever I want, to live as I choose, to say what I please, or to think what I want. These apparent freedoms, however, are not true freedom; they are consequences of true freedom.

10.3 Another Vision of Man

The vision of man that has been presented in the previous chapters assumes that man was created good. It also assumes that man disobeyed the Creator and, as a consequence, his nature is now flawed. One of the consequences of this flaw is that we find in ourselves a tendency toward selfishness, to use other people as a means to our own ends, and to use the appetites for purposes other than those for which they were created. The ultimate reason that explains the existence of evil is within us.

Another consequence of the flaw is that the original imprint of the moral law that was placed within us is now distorted. Looking into our inner self does not guarantee that we will always find immediately and without error what is right and wrong. The following is a good analogy.

The moon, falling on a perfectly still lake, will give a perfect image of itself; but let the lake be ever so slightly ruffled, and the image will be broken up into small pieces; let the lake be really ruffled, and the image will be no more than broken sparkles of light scattered here and there. It is still from the moon that these sparkles come, but no one looking at them could form a picture of the lovely luminous globe of the moon itself. Thus, even when the distortion is greatest, no man's nature is without some trace of God's law still imprinted; but it is not always easy to read.[2]

In addition to this vision, there are other ways of understanding what a person is. One of the most popular ones is what may be called the "individualistic" vision. This vision of man has three elements in common with the view that has been portrayed in this book:

1. Man was created good.

2. It is the inner self that makes each person unique and unrepeatable.

3. The truth about the human being is written in his heart; it is built into him. Therefore, in order to know what is right and wrong, man can look within his inner self to find that truth.

Despite these common elements, the individualistic vision of man assumes that human nature is not flawed (there was no original sin). In the primitive state of nature in which he was created, man was innocent and good, with no selfishness nor deceit. . . and he continued to be good.

If man is intrinsically good, how can we explain the evil that we see in the world? How can we explain the vanity, selfishness, ambition, and deceit that we see in the human heart? The answer is that man was corrupted by society.

In the original state of nature man was a savage, but he was innocent, noble, and uncorrupted. When he began to become civilized, the layers of rules and social conventions that were added to his life eventually made him lose his innocence. Man became concerned with power and money, and he began to base his behavior on egotistic calculation. It was civilization that made him selfish and corrupt.

For this vision of man, the origin of evil lies outside of man (in society). If it is society that corrupts man, the ideal solution would be to return to man's primitive state before the advent of civilization. Is such a thing possible in practice? Will man want to live again as a savage? Having played video-games, will he want to go back to the woods?

This solution (going back to man's primitive state as a savage) is not practical, but at least man can try to recover the voice of nature that he carries within himself. Because the truth about the human being is written in his heart, by looking inward man will find an inner compass which will tell him what is right and wrong.

When man looks into himself, why should the voice of nature provide the right answer? Because nature is not flawed. Our inner self cannot lie because it expresses nature, and the original state of nature in which man was created was good, and it is still good. The basic assumptions of the individualistic vision of man have important practical consequences:

1. Because human nature is good, all I need to do in order to know what is right in a particular situation, is to look inward and connect with my inner self. Whatever I see, it will be the right thing to do.

   Notice what has happened. Instead of comparing my behavior with the moral law to see whether it is right or wrong, the individualistic vision claims that what- ever my inner self tells me, that is what is right. In other words, the source of right and wrong is my in- ner self. The "I" has been enshrined as the ultimate reference of morality.

2. If the source of right and wrong is my inner self, then behaviors are no longer right or wrong. They are right or wrong *for me*. What is wrong for you may be right for me. "If that works for you, fine; but for me, what works is this other thing." And what is right for me to- day may be wrong for me tomorrow (it will all depend on what I discover in my inner self tomorrow). Right and wrong become relative to the person.

3. Because civilization has created so many conventions and artificial rules, one runs the risk of living his life according to the opinions, religious beliefs, tastes, and even dress codes of others. As each person has his own unique way of being human, man should consult no one but himself. Man should be true to himself, he should be "authentic."

Being authentic means that one should not imitate anyone else, and that one should not follow social con- ventions, nor the advice of parents or those in author- ity, nor religious beliefs, dress codes, or any other rules that civilization may want to enforce upon him.

Because one's inner self is the source of right and wrong, being true to oneself becomes the source of right and wrong. Being authentic is what determines whether a behavior is right or wrong. "If it feels good, then it must be right."

4. Because man is intrinsically good, if you have problems or difficulties, it is because you live in society. It is the

social ties and conventions that restrict your freedom to express yourself and be authentic. Overcoming evil means getting rid of anything that limits your capacity to express your inner self.

If you are married and the feelings have tapered off, you may feel that you are not in love anymore. What is the right thing to do then? Look into your inner self. If you feel that being true to yourself implies sticking to your wife, that is what is good for you; if you feel that being true to yourself means putting an end to the relationship, that is what is good for you.

In general, if you feel good about your commitments, then they are good for you. If any difficulty that stems from them limits your freedom, then you should get rid of them because they are the source of evil in your life. The notion of a permanent commitment has no meaning for the individualistic vision of man.

5. Because the supreme value for this vision is being true to one's inner self, the rights of the person stem from "whatever I want to do." If my inner self is telling me to do something, then I have the right to do it. And legislation should recognize these individual rights.

   What if a person wants to take another's property? The answer for the individualistic vision is that, if a person wants to behave in such a way, it is because society has forced him to do so (man is intrinsically good, it is society that corrupts him).

6. Because the existence of evil is a fact, in order to avoid chaos and live a peaceful and prosperous life, man needs to agree to limit his individual rights. This is the origin of the *social contract*. Citizens agree to limit their freedoms so that they may lead a peace-

ful existence and commerce may prosper. What rights can citizens give up in order to achieve prosperity and avoid chaos? Everything is negotiable.

Citizens may agree to define the speed limit on the freeways, but they may also agree to define the meaning of the universe, the concept of human existence, or the meaning of life. "At the heart of liberty is the right to define one's own concept of existence, of meaning, of the universe, and of the mystery of human life."[3]

For the individualistic vision, stealing is not wrong in itself, it does not damage the person. What this vision of man simply claims is that, at this point in time, stealing is illegal. Society has agreed that stealing should not be allowed because this is what the majority of citizens finds appropriate now. There is no concern for human dignity. Man is good, so why bother?

As is easy to see, a small difference in the way of thinking (the fact that human nature is not flawed) leads to very different conclusions. The individualistic vision of man has developed over the centuries through the work of many philosophers. The first one to articulate it was Jean Jacques Rousseau, who lived in the 18th century (1712-1778).

10.4 Building Theories

After stealing a laptop, Jack has two options. Either he acknowledges that he did wrong, or he builds a "theory" to justify his behavior. A theory that comes in handy is that, in stealing the laptop, he has been authentic because he has done what his inner self was prompting him to do.

As we saw in Section 4.1, a law of human behavior is that "one should do good and avoid evil." It follows from this law that no one can admit that he is doing wrong permanently. If Jack decides to go against the moral law, he will need to find a way of justifying his actions, for he cannot admit that he is doing wrong permanently. Jack will need to develop a theory to justify his behavior and, from that moment on, instead of living according to the principles that are written in his heart, the theory will become his guiding principle.

If you are a contractor and you have the chance to get cheap materials of dubious quality, it may come to your mind that the difference in quality with what you agreed with your client is not so great, that your client will never notice, that if you do not make extra money here you may not be able to pay your employees... You will quickly build a theory to justify that what you want to do is right.

We have to be aware of this tendency that we all find in ourselves. If we do not fight it, it becomes a habit that is then difficult to uproot. The virtue that we need to fight this tendency is sincerity. Being sincere with ourselves, calling things as they really are, helps us see reality as it is.

If a person who makes a wrong decision is not sincere with himself (if he closes the "eyes" of the intelligence to one aspect of reality), then he will justify further choices in that direction. After a while, seeing reality in that particular way will become a habit that will dictate the way he lives. How sincere we are with ourselves has a tremendous influence on which vision of man we adopt.

10.5 Choosing a Vision of Man

You cannot prove by reason that you were born of your parents—you know it by an act of faith in them or in the person who put your name down on the birth certificate. However, the fact that you cannot prove it by reason does not mean that you were not born from your parents, or that it is irrational to believe so.

If you go to a grocery store and you see a can with a label that says "Tuna," how do you know that the can actually contains tuna? You cannot prove it by reason. You are trusting the company that cans the fish. Would you say that you are irrational? The fact that something cannot be proved by reason does not mean that it is not true, or that it is irrational.

In the case of the individualistic vision, it cannot be proved by reason that human nature is not flawed. Nor can it be proved that our nature is flawed (we know of the existence of original sin through Scripture). Any vision of man is based on principles that cannot be proved by reason. How, then, do we choose between competing visions of man?

The individualistic vision is appealing because it claims that man develops as a person by being true to himself (by doing whatever he wants). The supreme value for this vision is authenticity, and everything else is subordinated to being true to oneself.

This stands in sharp contrast with the vision of man that has been presented in this book, which sees man frequently saying no to himself. The end goal of this effort, however, is to develop the virtues so that man becomes able to make a complete gift of himself. The supreme value for this vision of man is love.

If a man with a strong temper wants to avoid being fired from his job he had better stop quarreling and blowing up whenever things are not done his way. If he lacks the virtue, he will not be able to do so... and he will be fired.

The reason for restraining his temper might be higher than a purely professional one. He may want to have control over his temper in order to give himself to his wife and his children. If he struggles one day after another to overcome

3

his bad temper, he will develop a habit of self-mastery, so that when he feels like yelling at his wife or his children he will find it easier to control himself.

For a person with a strong temper it might be hard to say no to himself continuously in little things. His instinctive reaction will be to get enraged and blow up when things are not done his own way. His daily efforts to control himself may turn out to be hard, but the outcome is a greater freedom. Once he develops the habit, it will be easier for him to choose what is right. Something good that was not possible in the past (controlling his temper) becomes available through virtue. Virtue increases freedom.

The person who does not say no to himself will have an easier life in one respect, but he will not have the freedom to make a complete gift of himself. His life might be easier, but he will not be able to love truly. The effort to acquire and develop virtues is the price that we have to pay for the freedom of the gift.

Hopefully this chapter has helped you realize how the ideas that we have in our minds can influence the way we act so deeply. And how an incorrect notion of what a human being is can lead to behaviors that are incompatible with true love.

Notes

[1] U.S. District Court, *United States v. Reid.*
[2] F. Sheed, *A Map of Life* (San Francisco: Ignatius, 1994), pp. 95-96.
[3] U.S. Supreme Court, *Casey v. Pennsylvania*, 1992.

Epilogue

The notion that one can develop as a person has appeared frequently in this book. We have seen that personhood is not a static reality, but a dynamic one, and that this dynamism is related to our capacity to give. In these final pages, we will develop this idea.

The two faculties that distinguish man from animals are intelligence and will.[1] These two faculties are at the foundation of our inner lives, and allow us to do two things that animals cannot do, namely, to have and to give.

Looking at what we have, we realize that man can have at three different levels.[2]

I. *Man can have things externally.* For example, you may have a skateboard that you have built from scratch (it is the outcome of your doing), or you may own a patent (which is also the outcome of your doing), or you may have money in your bank account (which is the outcome of your work).

II. *Man can have things immanently.* The word "immanent" comes from *in-manere,* which in Latin means to remain within. Something immanent is something that stays within you, as opposed to something transcendent, which exists outside of you.

If you build a skateboard, the outcome remains outside of you. Immanent having is different. When you have an idea, you possess the idea in the act of knowing. Ideas "live" in your mind, unlike skateboards or patents, which "live" outside of you.

The outcome of an immanent action is not possessed as something external to the corresponding faculty, but is kept in the faculty itself. Memories are possessed in the act of remembering. Memories "live" in our memory, as opposed to a picture, which is an external object that has existence of its own, and "lives" outside of us. In the same way, our feelings are possessed in the act of feeling, and our fears are possessed in the act of fearing; when we hear a sound, we possess the sound in the act of hearing; when we smell the aroma of a flower, we possess the aroma in the act of smelling.

III. *Man can have virtues.* Each time our intelligence and our will are used, their inner structure is modified, so that they are perfected or become worse with respect to their object. The intelligence becomes more capable of pursuing truth, and the will becomes more capable of pursuing good. Virtue is the improvement of a higher faculty as a consequence of its own operation; vice is its worsening.[3]

The notion of virtue should not be confused with that of mechanical habits or routines (what in the social sciences is called "learning by doing"). The first time that one changes a diaper it usually takes a long time; but after doing it twenty times, one can do it much faster. When a person starts at a new job, everything is new and it takes him a long time to perform simple tasks; but once he has been performing a task for a long time, he acquires certain abilities and he is able to do it faster and more efficiently. If you work at a fast food restaurant, it will take you some time to learn how to prepare a hamburger, but once you acquire the routine you will prepare many hamburgers every hour.

This ability to perform mechanical tasks (whether manual or intellectual) is not virtue. Virtue has to do with perfecting the will and the intelligence with respect to their objects (good in the case of the will, and truth in the case of the intellect).

Each time we use our intelligence and our will they acquire stable dispositions. Parents repeat frequently to their children that "actions have consequences." This is a very deep truth that applies not only to children, but to everybody. Our good choices translate into virtues, and our bad choices into vices.[4]

One may get the impression that animals can also have externally and immanently. For example, when a bird builds a nest, it seems that it is not just one more nest, it looks like it is its own nest. When a dog bites a stick and holds onto it, the dog is in a sense appropriating the stick. It also seems that a dog has what it sees in the act of seeing, and what it smells in the act of smelling.

Animals, however, are not aware of a self (of an "I"). A dog can carry a stick in its mouth, see different colors and shapes, hear noises, and smell scents. These actions will generate images or impressions in the dog's brain, and its appetites will react to the sense impressions. But the dog is not able to reflect on itself and realize that there is an "I" behind these experiences; it cannot realize that these experiences (seeing, hearing, smelling, or carrying a stick) are happening "to me."[5]

Suppose that you have a rich uncle who, just before dying, orders a $10 million transfer to one of your bank accounts, and suppose also that, for whatever reason, you never check that particular account. The money would be in the bank, but during your life you would not be aware that you had it. It can thus be said that you never had the money, for you never took possession of it. Something analogous happens with animals. They cannot take possession of things because they do not know that they have them. In order to have something, there must be an "I" who has it.

As the faculty that allows us to know the existence of relations is our intelligence, it is this faculty that allows us to have. To say that man is a rational animal is equivalent to saying that man is an animal that can have.

A wealthy person has riches, but this is just external having. A person who has a good education has more than the person who has riches, for immanent having is of a higher order. And a person who has virtues has even more than the person who has a good education. The highest form of having is having virtues. (To be just is more important than being rich; to be honest is more important than being successful; to be pure is more important than being popular; to be truthful is more important than being famous).

Note that we do not have our "I", we are our "I". The "I" is not possessed. The "I" is what defines the subject who possesses things.

Let us now look at our giving. One of the operations of the will is to desire. When we desire, the will tends toward something that is not possessed (if you desire to own a Ferrari, it is because you do not have one). The fact that our desires point to something that we do not have manifests a certain lack, which is always an imperfection.

The Greek philosophers understood love as desire. Therefore, love was less perfect than having (desiring something
that we do not have is less perfect than having it). Because
virtue is the highest form of having, virtue was for them the
highest calling of man. For the Greeks, to be a good person
was to be a virtuous person.

Besides desiring, the will can also give. Man's giving can
be of two types:

I. *Man can give what he has.* To others we can give material things, money, ideas, time, knowledge, affections,
and so on. The more immanent the possession, the
more difficult it is to give.

II. There is one instance in which *man can give what he
does not have,* namely, man can give his "I". Giving the
"I" is different than the other type of giving because
we do not give what we have, but rather what we are.

Giving what we have has limits, while giving what we are
does not. The more you give yourself, the more of a person you become. Personhood is not static. We improve or
become worse as persons depending on how much we give
ourselves. A person who does not have the opportunity to
get a good education, or to travel much, or to know the cor-
porate world, but who gives himself completely, will develop
much as a person because he has loved much.

When we say that in order to give ourselves we first need
to possess ourselves, this has to be properly understood because we do not have our "I" (we are our "I"). To possess
ourselves means having control over our feelings, our appetites, and the rest of our faculties. And, as we already
know, we achieve this through virtue.

But one may be a virtuous person and still not know what true love is (the Greeks only saw half of the picture). To be a good person is to be a virtuous person who gives himself to others.

The Aristotelian definition of man as a "rational animal" is a good definition, but a poor description. As a good definition it allows us to neatly separate man from what is not man. For example, it allows us to distinguish man from goats (which are not rational), as well as from angels (which do not have a body). As a description, however, it is so poor because it leaves out so much. To be a "rational animal" is equivalent to being an "animal that can have," which leaves out the giving (it only describes half of the person).

Boethius's definition of the person as an "individual substance of rational nature" is also a poor description. Besides giving what he has, man can also give what he is, and it is precisely by giving his "I" that he develops as a person. This giving of the self is what lies at the core of personhood, but this is nowhere present in the above definition.

Boethius's definition is also static, while personhood is dynamic. It can only be so because the gift of self is a promise. Giving one's "I" requires an initial decision, which is one of the most important decisions in life, but carrying it out is something that we accomplish over time.[6]

The nature of a particular thing is what answers the question "What is this?" A human being, besides having a nature, also has an "I". Besides answering the question "What are you?" he can also answer the question "Who are you?" Nature is static; as long as a thing exists its nature does not change. Personhood, however, is dynamic. Depending on the quality of our love, we can become better or worse persons.

By the end of this book, you know more about true love. Knowledge, however, is just one more way of having. In the same way that on a cold winter's day you cannot get warm just by thinking about a good chimney fire, or in the same way that an athlete cannot win the gold medal just by thinking about his event, you will not be able to love just by thinking about true love. You need to practice.

San Diego, September 20, 2006
Barcelona, October 12, 2011

Notes

[1] "Rationality and the capacity to love are the most powerfully emblematic and most highly prized features of human nature. The former guides us most authoritatively in the use of our minds, while the latter provides us with the most compelling motivation in our personal and social conduct. Both are sources of what is distinctively humane and ennobling in us. They dignify our lives." See H. Frankfurt, *The Reasons of Love* (Princeton: Princeton University Press, 2004), p. 64.

[2] See L. Polo, *Sobre la existencia cristiana* (Pamplona: Eunsa, 1996), pp. 103-135.

[3] We say that the "object" of the sense of sight is color, of the sense of hearing is sound, and of the sense of taste is flavor. The object is what the particular power acts upon or is oriented to. It is in this sense that we say that the object of our will is *the good,* and that the object of our intelligence is *truth.*

[4] An incorrect choice may have external consequences, like going to jail, or getting infected with sexually transmitted diseases. These, however, are not the worst consequences of our actions. The worst outcome is that the inner structure of our intelligence and our will is damaged, and we becomes less capable of making good choices in the future. If you make money in a dishonest way, you may have more, but you *are* less.

[5] "Animals of various lesser species also have desires and attitudes. Perhaps some have thoughts as well. But animals of those species—at least, so it appears—are not self-critical. They are moved into action by impulse or by inclination, simply as it comes, without the mediation of any reflective consideration or criticism of their own motives. Insofar as they lack the capacity to form attitudes toward themselves, there is for them no possibility either of self-acceptance or of mobilizing an inner resistance to being what they are. They can neither identify with the forces that move them nor distance themselves from those forces. They are structurally incapable of such interventions in their own lives. For better or for worse, they are not equipped to take themselves seriously." See H. Frankfurt, *The Reasons of Love* (Princeton: Princeton University Press, 2004), pp. 17-18.

[6] That personhood is dynamic does not mean that we become persons over time, but rather that we develop as persons over time. Personhood is not an attribute that eventually emerges in the human being as the result of a development process, nor is it something that we have or acquire. It is what we are.

APPENDIX

The Biology of Conception

A.1 The Fertility Cycle

Knowing the biology of conception and the different phases of the fertility cycle can help us appreciate the beauty of human sexuality in a deeper way. It can also give us a better understanding of the meaning of the sexual union.

When a girl is born, she already has about one million eggs in her ovaries. No more eggs are produced during her lifetime. By the time she reaches puberty, about 300,000 remain. During puberty the eggs begin to mature and each month one egg ripens and leaves the ovary. The ovum (egg) passes through the fallopian tube and reaches the uterus. (See the figure on the following page). If the egg is fertilized by a sperm, gestation begins and the result is pregnancy. In this process we can distinguish several phases, which are controlled by different hormones secreted by the ovaries and other glands. The fertility cycle can be divided in the following four phases.[1]

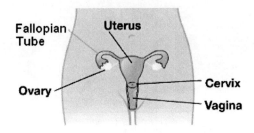

Adapted from www.nlm.nih.gov.

1. BEFORE OVULATION the ovaries secrete *estrogen,* a hormone that signals for an egg in the ovary to begin to develop and causes the lining of the uterus to thicken. This lining is composed of tissue (cells) and blood, and it forms a nourishing nest for the egg in the case it is impregnated by a sperm. Another important effect of estrogen is that, several days before the woman ovulates, a flow of *cervical mucus* starts in a small way. Let us look at the role of this mucus.

For the sperm to reach the ovum it has to go from the vagina into the uterus, through what is called the *cervix* (or cervical canal). Cervical mucus, produced by the cells in the lining of the cervix, helps a sperm reach the uterus and eventually impregnate the egg.

Fertile cervical mucus maintains the life of sperm, nourishes it, and allows it to pass freely through the cervix. In fertile mucus, sperm may live for up to three days, or in rare circumstances for five days or even longer. The start of flow of cervical mucus is a very positive sign that the fertile time of the woman has started. Cervical mucus can be recognized by sensation, by appearance, and by testing with the finger-tip.

2. OVULATION occurs when an ovum is released from the woman's ovary. The ovaries release a heavy surge of estrogen (causing the lining of the uterus to thicken and to get ready to host an egg if it were fertilized). Between 24 to 36 hours after the surge, the egg is released from the ovary to the fallopian tube and it begins to move toward the uterus.

As the estrogen level rises, the cervical mucus will become more profuse and it will give the woman a sensation of lubrication or slipperiness at the outer part of the vagina (the vulva). The appearance of the cervical mucus will be similar to that of raw egg white. Fertile cervical mucus is thin, watery, and transparent.

Once the egg is released, the ovaries begin to secrete *progesterone* (which means pro-gestation). The main function of progesterone is to support pregnancy, which it does in four ways: It inhibits other eggs from developing; it causes the Basal Body Temperature (BBT) to rise about half a degree (this temperature can be checked by the woman when she wakes up); it causes an increase in blood vessels to the uterine lining; and it thickens the cervical mucus.

The egg can be fertilized within 24 hours of release; after that it disintegrates. As the sperm can live in the cervical mucus for a few days, pregnancy is most likely to occur from having intercourse during the six days leading up to and including ovulation.

3. AFTER OVULATION. This phase usually lasts around 14 days (11-17 days). During this phase the cervical mucus disappears. The wetness that the woman felt in her vulva ends with ovulation, and there is an abrupt return to thicker, sticky cervical mucus or to complete dryness (no presence of cervical mucus).

This symptom reflects the presence of progesterone, which thickens the mucus, forming a plug at the cervix that acts as an impenetrable barrier to sperm. If the egg is not fertilized within 24 hours, the progesterone production is slowed down. After around 14 days (11-17 days), there is no longer enough progesterone to supply the uterine lining with blood, so the lining separates from the uterine wall and begins to decompose.

4. MENSTRUAL PERIOD. The blood system washes the lining away. The lining together with the blood are discharged through the woman's vagina. This discharge is known as the *menstrual period,* and it lasts from 3 to 7 days. Once the lining is washed away, the ovaries can release another egg (the progesterone level is low) and the cycle begins again.[2]

If the egg is fertilized, the menstrual period ceases for the duration of the pregnancy. Therefore, missing a period is a likely sign, though not a definitive one, that a woman is pregnant. When the egg is fertilized, the progesterone level remains high during pregnancy (it is also produced by the placenta).

This cycle manifests that the female reproductive system is a piece of art. It is remarkable how all the glands, hormones, and organs interact in such a synchronized way. It shows how sexuality is designed for conception.

Sometimes people say, "My girlfriend (or my wife) got pregnant by accident." Knowing how the female reproductive system works, it is easy to realize that pregnancy does not happen by accident. One gets hit by a bus by accident, but pregnancy is no accident. Pregnancy is not a sign that something went wrong, but rather that things went right. Pregnancy is a natural outcome of sexual intercourse.

A.2   Natural Family Planning

Natural Family Planning (NFP) refers to the practice of achieving or avoiding pregnancies according to an informed awareness of the woman's fertility.

The facts discussed in Section A.1 can help a woman get a precise idea of when she is fertile. First, the flow of cervical mucus generally starts in a small way several days before the woman ovulates; it is a very positive sign that her fertile time has started. About the time she ovulates, her mucus may be abundant.[3] After ovulation, the progesterone released by the ovaries causes the cervical mucus to thicken and disappear from the vulva.

Second, the progesterone released by the ovaries causes the woman's waking temperature to increase slightly but distinctly after ovulation. (See the graph on the next page).

After a woman's waking temperature has been well elevated for several days, while her mucus has been disappearing, the woman can conclude that she is infertile. This method of observing the mucus and the waking temperature as indicators of fertility is referred to as the *Sympto-Thermal Method* (STM) of Natural Family Planning.

This method does not take much time. A woman just needs a few minutes to take her temperature when she wakes up each morning, and during the day she takes a moment now and then to become aware of her cervical mucus. It gives the woman an accurate, day to day picture of her fertility.

The STM is not the same as what is called the *Rhythm Method*. The Calendar Rhythm Method, developed around 1930, was based on biological averages, and it was not very effective in the case of women with irregular cycles.

The STM, however, also works with irregular cycles. If a woman's fertile time comes earlier or later than usual, she knows about it because the start of her cervical mucus comes

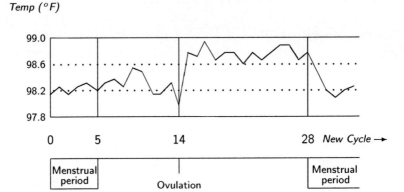

Waking Temperature Chart

earlier or later. The Sympto-Thermal Method can be used at above the 99 percent level of effectiveness for avoiding pregnancy (this is equal to the birth control pill and better than all the barrier methods).

A.3 Sexual Compatibility

Sometimes it is said that NFP makes sexual compatibility difficult, which may affect marriage in a negative way. Therefore—it is said—if husband and wife cannot responsibly have more children, they should use contraceptives in order to reinforce the stability and unity of their marriage.

In other occasions it is said that, marriage being such a big commitment, one should know beforehand if the man and the woman are sexually compatible, and this can only be known by having sex. The argument is oftentimes pre-

sented by saying that, in the same way that one does not
buy a car without taking it first for a test drive, it would
not make sense to marry a person without first having sex
with him or her, in order to ensure that there is sexual compatibility. What is the error in these arguments?

At the level of the person, we have seen that sex without
a permanent and exclusive commitment is a deep lie. And
we have also seen (in Section 7.4) how this lie reduces a
person's capacity to give himself completely, which is at the
foundation of what it means to be a person.

At a biological level, the previous question also has an
answer. When one gets sexually aroused, one experiences
increasing sexual pleasure until reaching climax, which is
called orgasm. In the case of males, this is ordinarily accom-
panied by an ejaculation of semen, and it is followed by a
period of detumescence or flaccidity, during which it is physi-
ologically impossible to experience a sustained erection. This
is called the *refractory period.*

Women are slightly different in two respects. On the one
hand, they do not get aroused as quickly as men. On the
other hand, after they reach orgasm, women do not have a
refractory period (or, if they do, it is a very short one), so
some women—unlike men—reach a second orgasm, or even
multiple orgasms.

This asymmetry in the refractory period implies that
the sexual union ends when the man reaches orgasm. But
the fact that the man reaches it, does not imply that the
woman does. If the man reaches orgasm first, the woman
does not enjoy the gratification associated with climax. In
other words, while the man always enjoys the sexual union,
the woman may not. If this happens frequently, the woman
may feel that she is being used. "He always enjoys it, but
I don't; it makes me feel as if I were his toy." This often
becomes a source of problems in marriage.

A couple is said to be *sexually compatible* when both enjoy the sexual union (when both reach orgasm). Ideally, husband and wife should do things in such a way that they reach it simultaneously. If they start penetration immediately, it is likely that the woman will not reach climax because women get aroused slower than men. The man has therefore the duty to control himself and prepare the woman by acts of tenderness, like kissing her or caressing the erogenous zones of her body (those that produce or are sensitive to sexual excitement).[4]

The need to prepare the woman is especially important if the couple is living periodic continence, for NFP requires them to abstain from intercourse around ovulation, which is precisely when the woman experiences higher sexual desire. This means that when she is not fertile and the couple can engage in sexual intercourse, the woman does not usually experience great sexual desire (she does not get aroused so easily). This requires the man to be even more careful about preparing his wife with tenderness and a long foreplay (not for hedonistic reasons, but for the good of his wife), facilitating in this way the satisfaction associated with climax.

> We have defined love as an ambition to ensure the true good of another person, and consequently as the antithesis of egoism. Since in marriage a man and a woman are associated sexually as well as in other respects the good must be sought in this area too. From the point of view of another person, from the altruistic standpoint, it is necessary to insist that intercourse must not serve merely as a means to allow sexual excitement to reach its climax in one of the partners, i.e. the man alone, but that climax must be reached in harmony, not at the expense of one partner, but with both partners fully involved...

Sexologists insist that the curve of arousal in woman is different from that in man—it rises more slowly and it falls more slowly. Anatomically, arousal occurs in the same way in women and in men (the locus of excitement is in the cerebro-spinal system at S2-S3). The female organism, as was mentioned above, reacts more easily to excitation in various parts of the body, which to some extent compensates for the fact that the woman's excitement grows more slowly than that of the man. The man must take this difference between male and female reactions into account, not for hedonistic, but for altruistic reasons. There exists a rhythm dictated by nature itself which both spouses must discover so that climax may be reached both by the man and the woman, and as far as possible occur in both simultaneously...

Non-observance of these techniques of sexology in the marital relationship is contrary to the good of the other partner to the marriage and the durability and cohesion of the marriage itself. It must be taken into account that it is naturally difficult for the woman to adapt herself to the man in the sexual relationship, that there is a natural unevenness of physical and psychological rhythms, so that there is a need for harmonization, which is impossible without good will, especially on the part of the man, who must carefully observe the reactions of the woman. If the woman does not obtain natural gratification from the sexual act there is a danger that her experience of it will be qualitatively inferior, will not involve her fully as a person...

In the woman this produces an aversion to intercourse, and a disgust with sex which is just as difficult or even more difficult to control than the sexual urge... Psychologically, such a situation causes not just indifference but outright hostility. A woman finds it very difficult to forgive a man if she derives no satisfaction from intercourse. It becomes difficult for her to endure this, and as the years go her resentment may grow out of all proportion to its cause. This may lead to the collapse of the marriage...

Precisely because a slower and more gradual rise in the curve of sexual arousal is characteristic of the female organism, the need for tenderness during physical intercourse, and also before it begins and after its conclusion, is explicable in purely biological terms. If we take into account the shorter and more violent curve of arousal in the man, an act of tenderness on his part in the context of marital intercourse acquires the significance of an act of virtue—specifically, the virtue of continence, and so indirectly the virtue of love.[5]

Leaving aside cases of illness, any healthy couple can be sexually compatible because it is a matter of "technique." Besides the foreplay, there are natural techniques that a man can use in order to delay ejaculation, and thus give the woman more time to reach climax. (Any gynecologist can explain this to a couple). The true compatibility that marriage requires is compatibility of giving, which requires enough virtues to ensure that the relationship between husband and wife is true love.

A.4   Effectiveness of NFP

There are several methods to determine the phases of a woman's fertility cycle. Each method relies on different indicators, like cervical mucus, ovulation pain, waking temperature, etc. Some methods use only one of these indicators, other methods use a combination of them.

In this section we discuss the effectiveness of the Sympto-Thermal Method. As we have seen, this method uses the cervical mucus and the waking temperature in a cross-checking way to determine the different phases of the fertility cycle. The information provided below proceeds from the references that are cited, as well as from John Kippley's article, "The Effectiveness of Natural Family Planning."[6]

Between 1976 and 1978, the U.S. Department of Health, Education, and Welfare conducted a study in Los Angeles to determine the effectiveness of two different systems of Natural Family Planning (the STM and the Ovulation method).[7] The number of volunteer couples that participated in the study was 1,247, with an average age of 28 and only one child per family (couples had been screened to eliminate those who had a serious reason to avoid pregnancy). The 1,247 couples were randomly assigned to one of the methods. Those that followed the Sympto-Thermal Method achieved a 100% use-effectiveness rate, i.e., zero unplanned pregnancies due to method failure. Note that this study was funded by the U.S. government, not by private groups.

In a study published in 1978, Dr. Josef Roetzer presented the results of the effectiveness of two methods of Natural Family Planning, one of them the STM.[8] Using a combination of three days of well elevated temperatures cross-checked by three days of disappearance of more fertile mucus, couples experienced zero unplanned pregnancies due to method failure in 17,000 fertility cycles, a 100% effectiveness rate.

Between 1970 and 1972, 1,022 couples participated in the Fairfield Study, a five nation study (Canada, Colombia, France, Mauritius, U.S.) in which a three day temperature-only rule was used (without cross-checking for the disappearance of cervical mucus).[9] The effectiveness rate was 99%.

This is just a sample of a variety of studies conducted in different countries, and under different conditions. Today it is firmly established that the Sympto-Thermal method is effective at above the 99% level.

This high effectiveness of the STM requires the couple to follow some relatively simple rules. In studies about effectiveness of contraceptives a distinction is made between unplanned pregnancies due to method failure, and unplanned pregnancies due to failure to follow the rules (or to inaccurate interpretation of symptoms). Even in the studies that reported a 100% use-effectiveness rate of the STM, a small number of pregnancies happened due to failure in following the rules established by the studies' protocols. In the study conducted in Los Angeles between 1976 and 1978 by Wade, McCarthy, Braunstein, et al., "none of the STM pregnancies were considered strictly method failures."

In order to use the Sympto-Thermal method one should consult specialized literature or attend a seminar by qualified instructors. What has been presented here is a basic description of the method, not enough to use it successfully. Excellent sources to start with are the websites of the *Couple to Couple's League* and *Family of the Americas Foundation*.[10]

Notes

[1] The information below is a brief summary of a variety of sources on reproductive biology.

[2] Following the menstrual period there may be several dry days, with no visible mucus (these days may be absent in short cycles and numerous in long cycles).

[3] Cervical mucus is nature's way of helping a man's sperm reach a woman's egg. In order to achieve pregnancy one needs three things: a good egg, good sperm, and good cervical mucus.

[4] These acts of tenderness are referred to as "foreplay." When a man cannot get aroused, or cannot maintain an arousal long enough to ejaculate, it is called erectile dysfunction (ED). The drugs that treat ED problems are meant to help men who cannot achieve an erection, or cannot maintain it long enough, have sexual intercourse (as it can be in the case of men who have diabetes, or those who are taking strong antidepressants, or older people whose testosterone level has decreased).

[5] K. Wojtyla, *Love and Responsibility* (San Francisco: Ignatius, 1993), pp. 272-275.

[6] See www.ccli.org/oldnfp/basics/effectiveness-p01.php.

[7] M.E. Wade, P. McCarthy, G.G. Braunstein, *et al.*, "A Randomized Prospective Study of the Use-Effectiveness of Two Methods of Natural Family Planning" in *American Journal of Obstetrics and Gynaecology* 141(4) (1981), pp. 368-376.

[8] J. Roetzer, "The Sympto-Thermal Method: Ten Years of Change" in *Linacre Quarterly* 45(4) November (1978), p. 370.

[9] F.J. Rice and C.A. Lanctot, "Results of a Recent Study of the Sympto-Thermal Method of Natural Family Planning" in *Linacre Quarterly* 45(4) November (1978), pp. 388-391.

[10] See *www.ccli.org* and *www.familyplanning.net*.

Bibliography

Aristotle. *Ethics*. London: Penguin, 1976.

Bonacci, M.B. *Real Love*. San Francisco: Ignatius, 1996.

Evert, J. *If You Really Loved Me*. Ann Arbor: Servant, 2003.

Evert, J. *Pure Love*. San Diego: Catholic Answers, 2003.

Frankfurt, H. *The Reasons of Love*. Princeton: Princeton University Press, 2004.

Gotzon, M. *Saber amar con el cuerpo*. Madrid: Palabra, 2005.

John Paul II. *The Theology of the Body*. Boston: Pauline, 1997.

Lewis, C.S. *The Four Loves*. New York: Harcout, 1960.

Plato. *Gorgias*. New York: Prometheus, 1996.

Polo, L. *Sobre la existencia cristiana*. Pamplona: Eunsa, 1996.

Schlessinger, L. *The Proper Care and Feeding of Husbands*. New York: Harper Collins, 2004.

Sheed, F. *A Map of Life*. San Francisco: Ignatius, 1994.

Sri, E. "The Law of the Gift". In: *Lay Witness* (September-October, 2005), pp. 24-25, 51.

Stenson, J. *Compass*. New York: Scepter, 2003.

Waiss, J.R. *Couples in Love*. New York: Crossroad, 2003.

West, C. *Good News about Sex and Marriage*. Cincinnati: Servant, 2004.

Wojtyla, K. *Love and Responsibility*. San Francisco: Ignatius, 1993.

Lightning Source UK Ltd.
Milton Keynes UK
UKOW050603260412

191466UK00002B/10/P